Spirited Voyager

A Memoir of Motherhood, Mission, and Ministry

by

Rev. Dr. Susan M. Hudson

Xulon Press

Xulon Press
2301 Lucien Way #415
Maitland, FL 32751
407.339.4217
www.xulonpress.com

Unless otherwise indicated, Scripture quotations taken from the Revised Standard
Version (RSV). Copyright © 1946, 1952, and 1971 the Division of Christian
Education of the National Council of the Churches of Christ in the United States of
America. Used by permission. All rights reserved.

Scripture quotations taken from The Message (MSG). Copyright © 1993, 1994,
1995, 1996, 2000, 2001, 2002. Used by permission of NavPress Publishing Group.
Used by permission. All rights reserved.

Printed in the United States of America.

ISBN-13: 978-1-6312-9689-5

Table of Contents

Sue with hands looking to heaven.

Dedication

*T*his story is my offering to God, who created me in my mother's womb, and who continued to nurture my faith from an early age. Many people from different communities of faith have befriended me along the way to expand my understanding of the breadth, depth, height and width of God's love for all of creation. My life belongs to the One who holds me in the present and the One who holds the future of all creation. The Spirit is bringing to fruition the gifts God has given me, while also leading me in unexpected and creative directions. This has truly been a "Spirited Voyage" with God's Spirit at the helm of my ship. She has introduced me to a wellspring of feminine wisdom for this ever-unfolding journey to the heart of God, who embodies mercy and love.

I dedicate this book to my mother, Mary Elizabeth Alsop Bower, who was a writer long before I was born. She infused me with a love for words and was my best editor. She loved me unconditionally and embodied the love of God with a feminine flair. She was a majorette in high school who twirled and tossed her baton with joyful laughter and danced the jitterbug during lunch breaks. Hers was not an easy life as a young child, nor as an adult, but she found joy and inspired joy in everyone who knew her.

She and my dad raised me to become all that God created me to be and I could not ask for anything more. My dad loved my mom and, in their later years, they did some wonderful traveling together. They went to Russia two times, Korea, and South Africa. Mom kept journals and pictures of the times they shared. They visited the wild ponies of Chincoteague, one of mom's dreams, and rafted down the Colorado River on Elderhostel adventures. They raised me, freed me and prayed blessings upon me, and now cheer me on from their heavenly home, where they reside with God and are eagerly waiting to share that resurrection chapter with me! Thank you, Mom and Dad, from the bottom of my heart!

Prologue

$\mathscr{L}$et me admit this fact upfront: being in water (oceans, lakes, rivers, pools, and even a bathtub full of bubbles) is where I feel most at home and free to be myself! My favorite memories as a child and teenager took place on rivers, in swimming pools and at water parks. Every summer, my church youth group took a trip to Ohiopyle where we rafted down a portion of the Youghiogheny River, or the "Yough" for short, which is a one-hundred-and-thirty-four-mile-long tributary of the Monongahela River in the states of West Virginia, Maryland, and Pennsylvania. Beginning when I was twelve years old, the minimum age required for participation, this trip was a high point of my year.

Each trip began with a brief orientation about how to navigate the river with three to six other raft-mates so that everyone would stay safe and be prepared for the unexpected. Guides rehearsed what to do if a person falls out of the raft. Never try to stand up. Recline on your life jacket and float on your back with your feet downstream until you are safely through the rapids and can swim to the side. Your feet are stretched out in front of you to help you bounce off rocks or other debris in the water.

At the memorial service for my ninety-nine-year-old Uncle Hank in January 2020, I reminisced with my cousins, Jeff and Roy, who had joined me on one of those raft trips in the late 1960s. Both fell out of the raft at the same time. We could feel their bodies glide under the raft, leaving my best friend, Marilyn, and me to guide the raft to a place where we could all be reunited.

As someone who loves poetry and metaphors, I am inviting you onto this spirited voyage with me, or a raft trip of reflection, about my life as a mother, missionary and minister. Will you be my traveling companion? There will be times we might need to laugh, cry, or swear under our breath, "What was she thinking?" I value intimacy and deep connections, so I thank you in advance for trusting me enough to climb into my vessel with me. As we bounce together through the rapids of my evolving faith journey, it is my hope and prayer that you will discover some nuggets of God's wisdom along the way. Collect a shell, a rock, a word, a seed, or a flower that can be planted, celebrated or might provide a source of light for your spiritual journey.

If you are burned out, used up, or broken in this season of your soul, I want you to know you are not alone. I wish it were true that people learn the most from their successes. However, in my experience, times of failure, loss, and disruption have taught me more about what it means to trust and lean into God's unconditional love and acceptance. As I share some stories of riding the rapids through my life, may God's love envelope you right where you are on your soul's journey. Let's put on our life jackets, grab our paddles, and trust God's Spirit to abide with us through the raging rapids that each one of us faces.

When we enter the quiet pools of contemplation in between the rapids, we will linger long enough to debrief, process, and learn from our experiences before moving forward down the river. Our rivers differ greatly, but we all benefit when we learn to integrate some spiritual practices to navigate the physical, emotional, mental and spiritual challenges in our lives. I invite you to climb aboard and tuck your feet into the spaces where the inflated sides of our raft meet the raft bottom. That will anchor us, as this journey begins. Where will you sit in our raft? The two people in front are more at risk of falling out of the raft when it hits a rock, a strong rapid, or a steep drop. The two people in the back have greater responsibility for steering the raft through the rapids. Perhaps you prefer the middle. No matter which seat you choose, welcome aboard! Please find your seat and anchor your feet as our journey begins.

"Seasons of the Soul"[1]

<hr />

[1] "Seasons of the Soul," was created by Stephanie E. Robinson in the early 1990s. It is a copyrighted piece of art, which Stephanie has given me permission to include. She is a self-taught artist who created this work during a difficult period of her life in her early twenties. You may learn more about Stephanie on her website: www.riverofmyart.com.

rebirth   fortitude   elation   symmetry   harmony   'movin' out'

Stephanie E. Robinson

RAFT #1:

Family of Origin

Chapter One

The Bower Family
Boat Embarks

*M*y earliest memories of family life are peaceful and full of love. My mother and father were active in the church, taking my brother and me regularly to Sunday school and worship. My father's parents had done the same for him, and we were raised in the same church where he was raised. However, it was the baptism of his children that rekindled my dad's faith in God and commitment to the church. Our community of faith, Mount Lebanon United Presbyterian Church in Pittsburgh, Pennsylvania, was where I was baptized, confirmed, active as a youth, employed on Summer Staff as a college student, married in 1980 and ordained as a Minister of Word and Sacrament in 1998.

Our family always sat in the front row of the far left balcony, overlooking the pulpit where the pastor delivered his weekly sermons. As a young child, I remember hugging Pastor Cliff after worship every Sunday. Althought it was a very simple, non-verbal gesture, I connected those hugs with God's love and imagined God as a round, smiling, bald man. Before Pastor Cliff moved to California to accept another call, he gave me a small picture of himself, which I carried in my wallet for years. Pastor Jerry, another favorite, read aloud *The Lion, the Witch and the Wardrobe,* by C.S. Lewis, during Children's Church.

Our church supported missionaries on a regular basis. A man from Kenya was hosted by our family when he visited our church. I can still remember him telling stories at our dining room table about his life, family and the unique challenges his church faced. One of my classmates, Sam Schreiner, had a mother who was raised in Pakistan, where her parents were also missionaries. During a monthly meeting for children during the worship hour called "Junior Missionary Society," Mrs. Schreiner told us many stories and showed slides of mission work in Pakistan. At one point in elementary school, I remember telling my mother that I wanted to grow up and become either a missionary or a heart surgeon.

As I grew older, Pastor Merl Galusha played guitar during youth group and challenged some of us intellectual high school cynics, who always sat in the back row at special events, to express ourselves. I remember writing him a story about my spiritual struggles and also some poetry. Marty Schreiner, one of Sam's older sisters, worked as the Director of Christian Education for several years and formed a leadership team of high school students who helped her plan and implement youth activities. She invited us to use our creativity and leadership in new ways, and valued our input.

Pastor Tim invited me, a high school student at the time, to preach at a Sunday night worship service for the whole congregation. I was honored and empowered when he entrusted that responsibility to me. I sat for hours in my bedroom, meditating on John 15, where Jesus invites his disciples to "abide in the vine." How does a person "speak for God" about a Scripture passage? As I meditated on Jesus' words, I wanted to understand what "abiding" in Christ would feel like. Although I had never driven a car with a manual transmission, I remember thinking that as long as one of your feet is on the clutch, the car will not move forward. Only a rhythmic, slow release of the clutch with one foot, while the other foot presses on the gas, allows the car to accelerate. In order to abide in Christ, I sensed that we need to let go of control in some way, and let go of our fears and insecurities, by pressing on the pedal of faith, if we want Christ's Spirit to live in us. Therefore, lifting my foot off the clutch would be like letting go of control of my own life; while, stepping on the gas would show my efforts to rely on the Holy Spirit, who truly fuels our Christian journey. My heart was always drawn to pastors, teachers, and mission- aries, because those people seemed to abide in Christ as I longed to do. The church was where I felt most at home, accepted and valued as a human being and child of God.

During those years, the ordination of women was still a controversial issue among church leaders and theologians. I distinctly remember a conversation I had with my fellow summer staff college students (all guys), and Art, a Ph.D. student, who was coordinating our summer of service. We were in Art's car, driving to Ligonier Valley Study Center to attend a Bible study on the book of Hebrews, taught by Dr. R.C. Sproul, who was a renowned evangelical teacher of the Bible. The guys were pointing out to me, with open Bibles in their hands, where the writer of Timothy made it clear that women should not teach or exercise authority in the church.[2]

When I arrived home later that night, I talked to my mother, raised in the Methodist Church, about the conversation. I said to her, "All of them were telling me that women should not be leaders in the church. I have no desire to pick that fight with them, but the truth is that I am smarter than all of them." Mom, always a peacemaker, laughed out loud and comforted me saying: "Honey, just trust God to lead you where God wants you to be. Don't let them discourage you."

Like my own mother, I do not like conflict. When I eventually did apply to seminary years later, I enrolled in a two-year program at Gordon-Conwell Theological Seminary, called a "Masters in Theological Studies," where I could avoid the ordination controversy and simply immerse myself in the study of Old and New Testament Scriptures in their original languages. Thankfully, I had the privilege of studying under Dr. David Scholer, who had written an entire book on why the ordination of women is biblically defensible. As a New Testament scholar and teacher, he deeply inspired me and opened up the Scriptures in liberating and refreshing ways, without undermining their authority or divine inspiration.

The beauty of the internet is the fact that with one Google search, I discovered a breath-taking testimony in memory of this mentor and teacher, whom I had not spoken to since 1980. In the journal, *Christian Feminism Today*[3], a tribute was written about Dr.

---

[2] I Timothy 2:12

[3] Anne Linstatter, *Christian Feminism Today*, Summer 2008 (Volume 32, Number 2).

Scholer's legacy: "Let it be known that one man on the evangelical side of the fence spent a lifetime working to give women access to Christian Ministry." The author continues: "For thirty-six years at four seminaries he taught 'Women and Ministry in the New Testament and the Church Today,' explaining that a careful reading of the gospels and letters of Paul demands full inclusion of women in church leadership. He mentored many women students and friends as they became pastors."

As a Baptist, Scholer publicly worked against the idea that women should be silent in churches, a position which is, unfortunately, still upheld in some churches. He was honored at the Evangelical and Ecumenical Women's Caucus' thirtieth-anniversary national conference, "for thirty-two years of service to biblical feminism." In an editor's note to the article, readers are encouraged to read Scholer's article, "My Fifty-Year Journey with Women and Ministry in the New Testament and in the Church Today."[4] Thank you, Dr. Scholer, for mentoring and empowering me as a woman in ministry!

---

[4] Dr. David Scholer, *Christian Feminism Today*, 2006 Issue.

Questions for Reflection:

➤ *Where have you felt most welcome, comfortable, loved and at home in this world? If the word, "raft," or "vessel" does not describe that place for you, what "place/ space" do you picture in your mind?*

➤ *Did you grow up in a place where you felt spiritually rooted, grounded and secure, or did you feel adrift, without a life-preserver, or a place of belonging?*

Chapter Two:

Falling Out of the Bower Family Boat

My family life outside the church had its ups and downs. I faced my earliest challenge as a five-year-old when I developed undiagnosed internal hemorrhaging. On top of that, I tested positive for measles and had to be put in the isolation ward at Children's Hospital in Pittsburgh. My mother sat outside the door to my room, reading me stories for hours. When people sent me gifts to entertain me while I was in isolation, I refused to play with them until I got out of the hospital, because anything I touched while I was there would be burned to prevent the spread of infection. I was more interested in the long term value of having many years to play with them! When my veins were collapsing and the doctor had to take blood from my neck, that was the straw that broke my back and made me cry. However, my mother's loving presence hovered over that whole bad memory.

School was a place where I thrived after I weathered the initial shock of not being chosen for the gifted group of second graders, who had the privilege of being called out of class to study French on a regular basis. My second-grade teacher labeled me a hard worker, but not particularly gifted. Looking back, I imagine I was a shy child, who listened a lot, absorbed what was going on around me, but did not draw attention to myself. Fortunately, at church, I participated in a drama club on Wednesday afternoons where I was chosen for fun roles in many of their productions: as Winnie the Pooh in one, the King (in a play for which I cannot remember the name), and many others. Though quiet and shy to most observers, when the ladies at church put me on the stage, I lit up and rose to the challenge, putting my heart and soul into whatever role they gave me.

My mom fell out of our family's boat emotionally when her only sister, Doris Alsop Moorman, died unexpectedly at age forty-four from a massive heart attack. She and my mother were extremely close and had already lost both their mother and father, when their parents were only in their fifties. My mom looked up to her glamorous older sister, as she dressed up to go out on dates in her high school years. Doris, called "Dook" by her family, wanted to be an actress, and my mother wrote stories about her. She had a son in her first marriage and two daughters in her second. When Aunt Doris and her family moved to Florida, when I was very young, our families became even closer. She and her two daughters came and stayed with us every summer for several weeks. Our summers together were full, fun and festive. We went horseback riding and visited the zoo, museums and theaters. We played board games and outdoor sports and ate summer dinners on our back patio, enjoying each other's company for weeks at a time. We felt like a family of seven!

When my aunt died in January of 1966, it was a sudden end to all those good times. Doris' son, Jim, got married in the fall of 1965, but due to financial constraints, my mother missed her nephew's wedding in Florida. She never dreamed it would have been the last time she would have seen her sister in person. She deeply regretted that decision. I joined my family on my first airplane flight to attend Aunt Doris' funeral in Ft. Lauderdale. I remember looking out the window at the kingdom of clouds outside the plane and feeling that I was closer to God than I had ever been before, but I also realized that death could strike at any time. It was a rude awakening.

My cousin, Barbara, was in seventh grade and her sister, Merry Lee, in ninth grade. Their lives were never the same after their mother died. Merry Lee had been with her mother at a school basketball game the night before and had gone to bed a little disgruntled that her mother had been reading a book rather than watching the game. The next morning her mother was gone. Her body had already been picked up by the undertaker before the girls woke up. My mother's grief was profound. For many years, my mother reached out to her nieces and nephew, keeping up with how they were doing. Their dad married a woman in less than a year, who turned out to be an alcoholic. My cousins struggled physically, emotionally, mentally and spiritually for many decades. As much as my mother tried to support her nieces, she could not replace the love of their mother. I learned by watching, as their lives unfolded, that I never wanted to take for granted the life of someone you love.

Questions for Reflection:

➢ *What are some memories in your childhood that were turning points, when you or someone you love fell out of your raft?*

➢ *How did the people you love work together (or not) to regain stability and make it safely through those rapids?*

Chapter Three

Rocking the Bower Family Boat

As an adolescent, I struggled with weight and low self-esteem. A young guy in my neighborhood, while I was in elementary school, gave me the nickname, "Ten Ton Tub," and my good friend, Lorinda, "Bean Pole." I would have happily traded nicknames with Lorinda. During my first year of junior high school, a new family moved in across the street from us. They had a daughter my age, who had clearly been living life in the fast lane in her previous neighborhood. When she invited me out on a blind date with her and her boyfriend, the person with whom I was being matched up rejected me at first sight. It was a very low blow to my confidence. During the summer between seventh and eighth grades, I went on the Weight Watchers diet with my mother and lost thirty pounds. I went from a size fourteen to a size four: a huge boost to my self-esteem.

Sadly, body image is critically important for young women in their teenage years. I continued to go up and down on the scale because my mom was a wonderful baker of desserts and my dad did not think a meal was complete without dessert. My strength was in academics, so I put most of my energy into my studies.

During my junior high years, I struggled to find a circle of friends that were good for me. At an overnight birthday party at one girl's house, she invited me into her kitchen, when her parents were out, and served me a glass of straight gin. I had never tasted alcohol at that point in my life and had no clue how much it would affect me. For the rest of that party, I can barely remember what happened, only that I was ashamed of myself and resented that the girl who hosted the party put me in that position. Unfortunately, to compensate for my low self-esteem socially, I did continue to dabble a little more into alcohol and drugs, because it helped me fit in and took the edge off of my social awkwardness.

Fortunately, my connection to the church helped me navigate those rough waters. I remember driving one of my best friends to the church parking lot after we were smoking marijuana. I asked her to come into the sanctuary of the church where we sat in the darkness and silence. After sitting for a while, she asked, "Can we leave yet?" I felt safe in God's presence and was reluctant to leave. My participation in the youth ministry at my church helped give me the strength to put some of those temptations behind me.

Questions for Reflection:

➢ *What circumstances or events during your adolescent years led you towards a dangerous waterfall?*

➢ *Were you able to change direction towards safer waters, or did you go over the waterfall, and what were the consequences?*

Chapter Four:

Being Launched from the Bower Boat

One of my coming-of-age moments after my junior year of high school was the opportunity to serve on a one-month summer work crew at Saranac Village, a Young Life Camp in upstate New York. A person had to be an active participant in weekly Young Life meetings, as well as a regular in their small group Bible studies, called "Campaigners." We were asked to read selected Christian books and attend discipleship classes. When it came time to embark for Saranac, I met someone on the van ride who became a close friend. Ken poured out his life story to me during the trip. We stayed connected throughout the month and continued our spiritual friendship for years afterward.

My job was in the kitchen as an assistant cook while Ken hooked the enviable job of serving as a lifeguard. Although we all worked ourselves to death physically during that month, the spiritual depth of our Bible studies, fellowship and the way we served each other sacrificially was my first taste of a close-knit spiritual community of people my age. If there were any of us on the work crew who were not finished with their job at the end of the day, the whole team pitched in to help. When it came time to leave the camp at the end of the month, I was devastated. Living in an intentional Christian community was a taste of heaven. I also developed the spiritual practice of studying the Bible on my own and journaling about my experiences. Ken ended up joining a Catholic charismatic community while he attended the University of Michigan, which led us in different directions.

Returning for my senior year of high school, I had the privilege of being asked to serve as the Editor-in-Chief of the school literary magazine, *The Unicorn*. My Advanced Placement English teacher during my junior year, the faculty supervisor, selected me for the position; however, she had to take sick leave that year. She had given us regular creative writing assignments during the previous school year, which was my favorite activity in her class. She did not give our work letter grades for the creative assignments, simply checks or check-pluses. Poetry soon became my life-line to express my deepest feelings and experiences. The art editor for the magazine, Tracy Franks, became my right-hand man throughout the year. His dream was to attend the United States Naval Academy. In addition to his incredible gifts as an artist, he was an accomplished drummer. He played for the school and also for a small group that did re-enactments of revolutionary war music at historical sites. Tracy eventually accompanied me to my senior prom (since he was one year younger). We dated the summer after I graduated from high school and it was difficult to say goodbye when August of 1973 arrived. Tracy accompanied my mom and me, when she dropped me off and said goodbye for my freshman year of college.

After wrestling with God a great deal during my senior year of high school, as I tried to discern the right place for myself, I chose to attend Wake Forest University in Winston-Salem, North Carolina. It was one of the biggest decisions of my life and my parents did not push me in any direction. Since my family had never moved, I was restless to go somewhere I had never been before. My dad was a college football referee on the side, which was his favorite hobby. One of our family vacations every fall centered around a college football game, where we tailgated, went out to fun restaurants with the other officials and their spouses or families, and sat mutely in the stands, hoping that there were no controversial calls by the referee! It was the weekend of dad's working the Army-Navy game at Veteran's Stadium in Philadelphia when I made the final decision to attend Wake Forest the following year. Dad was a little disappointed since he had introduced me to so many college campuses closer to home.

Since we had never moved and my parents' closest friends were their college buddies from Westminster College in New Wilmington, Pennsylvania, I felt like it was now or never to chart a new course and have the courage to get out of my comfort zone. I wanted to take a giant leap of faith and start a new life with a whole new set of friends. The South attracted me as a place where the pace might be a little slower. I had worked hard in my public school with its very high standards of academic achievement. My goal was to branch out and learn some life skills at college, rather than devoting all of my energy to jumping through more academic hoops. The final deciding criteria was that Wake Forest had a synchronized swimming club. I had been introduced to water ballet as a Girl Scout, so I could not wait to expand my horizons at the college level.

When it was time to make the "leap of faith drive" to Winston-Salem in August 1973, it turned out to be more excruciating than I imagined. I was severely homesick for at least two or three weeks. I could not sleep or eat well and wondered why I had decided to go there. I was leaving behind my boyfriend, Tracy, whom I had not been dating when I made the decision to go so far away to college. Instead of excitement about the new adventure, I was dissolving in tears. I arrived early to attend a pre-school retreat sponsored by the university; however, I learned early on that, for the most part, only North Carolina residents participated in this event. When they showed a silent movie of Sherman's troops burning Atlanta and everyone stood on their seats to cheer the Confederate army, I wondered what had led me there. For me, the Civil War was a chapter in my high school history book, but I discovered that the students around me that day called it, "The War of Northern Aggression."

Having been assigned a single room disappointed me at first since the stereotype of college always included a roommate. Living in a single room did not inhibit me from developing good friendships that first year and, in fact, it became a running joke with my closest friends, who gave me a Peanuts card which said: "No problem is so big or so complicated that it cannot be run away from!" I think they were a little jealous that I had a nice quiet space to retreat to whenever I needed privacy.

I attended an informal Fellowship Group on campus. I also visited different churches, Presbyterian and Baptist primarily, but I also explored some charismatic experiences with Pentecostal friends because I came to feel that my faith might have been a little too academic and cerebral. I prayed for the Holy Spirit to deepen my faith beyond my intellectual understanding. The energy and fervent prayers of my Pentecostal partners inspired me to deepen my relationship with the Holy Spirit.

Questions for Reflection:

> ➢ *Was there a distinct time in your life when you pulled your raft out of the river you knew best and put the raft on a river you had never navigated before?*

> ➢ *Did you ever second-guess the choice of that particular river and those raft mates, who paddled differently than you were raised to paddle?*

The College Raft Trip and Beyond

*M*y years at Wake Forest were rich in providing new experiences and allowing me to nurture life-long friendships. I went from being a German major to an English major at a critical moment of discernment. I had applied for a year-long scholarship to the Free University of Berlin. However, during the interview process, the German professors and the Dean questioned my Christian faith, implying that I was naïve, wondering aloud if I could handle myself in the challenging urban environment of Berlin. I left the interview feeling disrespected and made the decision to change my major to English.

Before long, I had enrolled in an overseas trip for the January term to England, Ireland and Scotland to focus on creative writing. My final paper was a take-off on Chaucer's *Canterbury Tales*, only my characters were inspired by all of the people in our group. The journey we took was a pilgrimage to the historic sites where Wordsworth, Yeats, Joyce, Shakespeare and other British, Irish, and Scottish authors did their work.

Later in the school year, the Chairman of the German Department stopped me on campus and asked me when I wanted to set up my course schedule for next year at the Free University of Berlin. I was stunned and told him I would get back to him. I called home and discussed the situation with my parents, expressing the fact that I had never been informed that the department had granted me the scholarship, and my life had taken a sharp turn in a different direction. I went the next day to the Department Chair and told him that I did not want the scholarship.

Forty-two years later, I attended an Alumni Gathering with couples who had met at Wake Forest. The first person I met at the event was a retired German teacher and graduate of Wake Forest ten years earlier than me. When she told me that she had also been a German major, we talked about the scholarship to the Free University of Berlin, which she had applied for during her college years. She was informed that because she was a woman, they could not give it to her. We laughed so hard. She was glad to hear that I had broken that barrier. Over the years, I have sometimes wondered how my life would have been different if I had spent that year abroad.

One of my favorite activities in college was being part of the synchronized swimming team. We did one or two shows every year, utilizing underwater speakers to project our music under the water so that we never missed a beat. We did the music from *"South Pacific"* during my senior year, while I was president of the club. In that final show, I had the opportunity to swim a solo, starting with a cartwheel off the diving board, to the song: "Honey Bun." My parents came down from Pittsburgh to see the show. Unlike my dad, who always favored speed and competition, I loved the beauty and teamwork of synchronized swimming. While at Wake

Forest, I also completed my Water Safety Instructor Certification with the faculty supervisor for the synchronized swimming club.

As I neared graduation from college with an English major and a Secondary Teaching Certificate, I was feeling called to seminary, but my father informed me that I needed to get a job. My roommate and I were offered teaching jobs in Virginia Beach. "Teach at the Beach" signs, which Virginia Beach Public Schools posted on our campus, effectively lured us in that direction. Some last-minute sentimentality about leaving Winston-Salem led me to take a summer job as a lifeguard and swim coach before moving to Virginia Beach.

Questions for Reflection:

➢ *How do you make transitions from one "raft" to another in your life? Do you need to do it quickly without looking back, or do you take your time in saying goodbye?*

➢ *When have you fallen into a new "raft," almost by accident, and discovered new adventures with a whole new set of raft mates?*

RAFT #2:

Family of Choice

Building the David and Sue Hudson Family Vessel

*M*y dad's parting words to me when I first left for college were: "You are probably going to end up marrying someone from down there." Sure enough, he was right. How do I sum up the adventure of finding my rafting partner for life and ministry, David Lindsay Hudson? We might have missed each other if God had not been the choreographer of our courtship. We met (two life-long Presbyterians) at a Baptist University. David and I attended the same campus Fellowship Group on Sunday nights, and that was where I built my closest friendships. My roommate junior year was Mary Gamble, a native of Charlotte, where David's family also lived. Since she had a car, and neither David nor I did, we rode to church most Sunday mornings together, attending a Presbyterian Church in town. I will never forget one Sunday morning when Mary discovered that her tire had gone flat. David arrived at our dormitory dressed in his Sunday best, not knowing we had a problem. He rolled up his sleeves and had that tire changed without missing a beat. Cool guy, I thought. Very impressive. David had dated several of my friends, so I never thought much further about him.

David and I connected again when David's older brother was getting married in Charlotte during the same weekend two good friends from college were getting married there. Since it was the week before Christmas in 1976, David, Mary and I departed from Wake Forest together to attend these events. I had booked myself an airline ticket from Charlotte to Pittsburgh to visit my family over the remainder of Christmas break. After the weddings were over, David offered to accompany us to the airport. When we picked David up at his house, we met his parents for the first time. In David's family, it was very common to give guests and visitors gifts. David asked his dad to find me a little gift before we left for the airport. David's dad worked for Belk Stores and loved flea market and yard sales, so he always had potential gifts for whomever stopped by the house. Although it was wrapped, David cautioned me that it was fragile, so I had better not drop it. As the story gets told and re-told, it is said that David told his Dad that he "kind of liked me," and wondered if his dad had a gift he could give me. That simple mug has traveled the globe with us.

"The Cup"

Five months and no dates later, I was ready to graduate from Wake Forest. At the last minute (*Thank you, God!*) I decided to linger for the summer in Winston-Salem rather than returning to Pittsburgh. I accepted a job as a swim coach and lifeguard at Pine Brook Country Club and moved into an apartment with an acquaintance from college. Right next door was another college friend who happened to be dating David Hudson. We met and greeted each other and I learned that David was planning to finish up a few courses at the University of North Carolina in Charlotte, but changed his mind at the last minute to stay on campus and finish at Wake. (*Thank you, God!*) The first week I moved into my apartment, I learned David and his girlfriend had broken up.

David enjoyed visiting me at the Country Club pool where I worked and would often bring his reading assignments. I offered to teach him a thing or two about sailing when I learned that one of his friends owned a sunfish, a type of sailboat. Another one of our annual Bower family vacations had been to Deer Valley YMCA Camp, where my dad spent most of his time sailing in a sunfish with me as his crew. I also worked as a volunteer at that camp one summer during high school, where I was assigned to work as a lifeguard for the swimming area of the lake and assisted with the sailboats.

David invited me to visit his family in Charlotte a few times, where we enjoyed bicycle rides around Charlotte neighborhoods. By the time the summer was over, I was getting ready to move to Virginia Beach. David accompanied me to Pittsburgh at the end of the summer, and also helped my brother and his wife move from Chapel Hill back to Pittsburgh, before helping me move to Virginia Beach. When we arrived in Virginia Beach with my bedroom set from Pittsburgh, Mary Gamble took one look at the two of us and knew we were no longer just friends.

That began a three-year long-distance court-ship between Charlotte and Virginia Beach, then between Venice, Italy and Virginia Beach, and eventually between Gordon-Conwell Theological Seminary in South Hamilton, Massachusetts and Princeton Theological Seminary in New Jersey. Both of us were called to mission and ministry, but when would our lives realign again?

For someone who loves learning languages, my summer of study at the Summer Institute of Linguistics in Seattle, Washington, and then two years at Gordon-Conwell were long drinks of refreshing water. Seriously studying the Scripture in the original languages, along with doing contextual and historical studies in a seminary community with others who shared that interest, was invigorating and life-giving for me. The first year, I lived with a family I had known in Pittsburgh and, the second year, I lived in an apartment with other female friends, who later became bridesmaids!

Both of our families wondered why David and I did not choose to attend the same seminary. David's older brother, Harold, was at Gordon-Conwell, so David and I visited each other back and forth for two years. The summer after our first year of seminary, I moved to Charlotte to spend one more summer as a lifeguard. I lived with an older woman in his parent's neigh-borhood. David did a summer ministry internship at Westminster Presbyterian Church. There, we facili-tated children's messages in worship for the first time together. We truly enjoyed being in the same town for several months, and at the end of the summer, David and I made plans to get married.

With an engagement ring on my finger that I inherited from my jovial, great Aunt Isabel, who had no children of her own, we each returned to our respective seminaries, knowing that the end of our long-distance relationship was in sight. I sped up my studies and moved home mid-year to plan a wedding in Pittsburgh with my family. Meanwhile, David and I applied and were accepted to serve as Volunteers in Mission for the Presbyterian Church (USA), in between his second and third years of seminary. We applied and were accepted as an engaged couple and had to raise our financial support through our church families and friends, which was easy to do.

While at home with my family, I asked David to go to a counselor with me before we got married. The counselor advised me that I was not quite ready to get married, but we had already been accepted as Volunteers in Mission with the Presbyterian Church (USA) as fiancées and were scheduled to serve in Seoul, Korea, a month after our wedding. I had some fears but informed the counselor that I could not bear to let David go oversees without me again. Ready or not, I was going!

We were married on June 7, 1980, right after I graduated. David's brother, Harold, gave us a charge at our wedding, comparing us to "Priscilla and Aquila," a missionary couple in the New Testament, who were friends of Paul. From the start, our lives were oriented towards serving God together, wherever that might lead us. Within a few weeks after our wedding, we moved into the McCallum House at Montreat Conference Center, along with a houseful of other mission co-workers, to be oriented and trained for mission service. Our first year of marriage was not just a leap of faith into our commitment to each other; it was also a leap of faith into missionary life and Korean culture. There were moments of deep loneliness for me, but also times of great excitement and adventure. If it sounds like a "whirlwind," that is exactly how it felt. David is a man on the move and rarely looks back to make sure everyone is able to keep up with him. I wanted to be part of that exciting dance!

Having grown up in a household with two brothers, David learned to eat fast, before the food ran out. The three boys engaged in many escapades in the neighborhood, that their parents only learned about later, when they told the stories. David had a newspaper route and then worked at a gas station, because he is not someone to let grass grow under his feet. He was raised to be a hard worker: any kind of yard work, cleaning gutters, planting bushes. His family also owned some rental property at the beach, which David remembers more as a work project than a place for family vacations.

David does most of his processing of thoughts and feelings internally, so my ups and downs emotionally during the cultural adjustments were hard for him to understand. I imagine that was what the counselor had observed about us. David is a "doer," who will stop at nothing to accomplish a task. I am one who feels deeply and needs to talk about her feelings to process and manage them in a healthy way. There were very few people or girlfriends in whom to confide as a newly married missionary woman. However, I did find a mentor, named Vonita Spencer, who became a spiritual mother to me. She was a woman of deep prayer and also an artist, who would make time for me and pray for me regardless of the circumstances. I remember going to her home on Easter afternoon, interrupting her family's Easter dinner; however, she graciously ushered me into a private bedroom, prayed with me, as I cried, and did not miss a beat while hostessing her guests. During that year, I also learned to depend on God in a deeper way. The Hudson Family Raft was first put into the waters, metaphorically, in the Han River in Seoul, Korea.

In 1980, the political situation in South Korea was tense. President Park Chung-hee had been assassinated in December 1979. Prime Minister Choi Kyu-hah had taken the president's role, only to be overturned six days later by Major General Chun Doo-hwan through a military coup d'état. In May of 1980, masses of university students and labor unions led strong protests against authoritarian rule throughout the country. Chun Doo-hwan declared martial law on May 17, 1980, and protests increased.

On May 18, a confrontation broke out in the city of Gwangju between students and government forces dispatched by the Martial Law Command. The incident lasted nine days and resulted in what is known as the Gwangju Massacre. The civilian death toll was nearly two-hundred, with eight-hundred-and-fifty injured. In September, 1980, only weeks after David and I had arrived in Seoul for the first time, President Choi Kyu-hah was forced to resign with the new military leader, Chun Doo-hwan, taking charge of South Korea's military government. On several occasions, I remember taking pictures of the military troops that surrounded the seminary campus where David and I were assigned to serve.

On a more positive note, our first year of marriage in Seoul exposed us to one of the fastest-growing churches in the world! As newlyweds, we moved into a student dormitory on the seminary campus, and the first question I was asked by a student who lived in the same building was, "How many hours do you pray every day, Mrs. Hudson?"

"Hours?" I stuttered. "Uh, hmmm, let's see. I am not sure I ever tried to count before…"

The Presbyterian Church of Korea had a deep commitment to prayer, which is a legacy shared by all of the Christian communities in Korea. We studied the history of Christianity in Korea and experienced their fervent spirituality in real-time, which included prayer meetings, called: "Saebyok kido hai" at five o'clock every morning. If pastors think their responsibilities are great in the United States, imagine meeting your parishioners every day at that time of the morning! Many more women than men attended those prayer gatherings, since the men worked outside the home. However, men and women often poured out their hearts and souls in their prayers, which could happen simultaneously, rather than one person at a time.

As for retreats, the seminary students loved to go to the "prayer mountain" to study the Bible, worship and pray long into the night. I found it delightful that when seminary students finished their final exams, they did not go to pubs or taverns, but journeyed to prayer mountains to deepen their faith beyond their book knowledge! Alcohol consumption was not a part of their spiritual practices or personal habits! The depth and fervency of their spiritual lives impacted me in a positive way. I also grew to understand that their long years of suffering, war and oppression from foreign powers had provided opportunities, or cauldrons of transformation, to deepen their spiritual resilience and strengthen their trust and reliance on God alone, rather than human institutions. I often give credit to my years in Korea as the place where prayer became a cornerstone in my own life.

Questions for Reflection:

> ➢ *Where was your career raft first launched? How did that first assignment utilize and/or stretch your spiritual gifts and talents?*

> ➢ *What people were in the raft with you and what did you learn from them, as you paddled together in this new river? Did you splash each other every once in a while to get his or her attention?*

Together is Better!

*A*fter one year as Volunteers in Mission, we returned to Princeton for two more years of education. The first year we lived with Dr. Sam and Eileen Moffett, missionaries in Korea, who had retired the year we were volunteers. Sam became David's supervisor while he completed a Masters of Theology (Th.M.) degree in Missiology. The second-year we lived in an apartment with international students who were attending the seminary. Our closest friends were Africans and Indonesians. During those two years, I worked as a secretary at Princeton University in the Department of Art and Archaeology and also completed a Master's degree in Christian Education, taking advantage of the rich academic and spiritual atmosphere. I attended classes at the seminary during my lunch hour, evenings and in summer school.

David and I returned for a four-year missionary appointment to Seoul, Korea, at the same seminary where we had lived as volunteers. I will never forget the plane flight back to Seoul in 1983, exactly one week to the day after the downing of a Korean Airlines Flight 007 on September 1, 1983, which took the same flight path as the one we were taking the following week. KAL007 was a scheduled flight from New York City to Seoul, via Anchorage, Alaska. The flight was thought to have veered off course and was shot down by a Soviet SU-15 interceptor. While on that same route one week later, I was reading a magazine article about the downing of the plane the week before. The story recounted that the passengers' last announcement from the cockpit was an announcement that they were three hours from Seoul's Gimpo International airport and the crew would be serving breakfast and beverages shortly. When our breakfast was served to us, not long after I read that article, it was another haunting reminder of life's fragility. I took time to pray for those devastated families, who had lost loved ones and were still in shock from that tragic flight. What actually happened on that fateful flight was never fully revealed until the end of the Cold War, when the Soviet Union was dissolved.

One of David's primary responsibilities at the Presbyterian Seminary was overseeing a Graduate Program for Third World Church Leaders, offered in English, as part of the Korean Seminary's mission-outreach to church leaders in developing countries. While in Korea, I also built relationships with those church leaders who had become our community of faith while we lived there. I also taught English, New Testament studies, attended "Trés Dias" for spiritual growth, and became a part-time Christian educator for Seoul Union Church, where I was invited to preach my first sermon on the mission field.

Questions for Reflection:

> ➤ *Describe a time in your life when a tragedy in someone else's life struck a deep chord in you.*

> ➤ *When have you had the opportunity to share the same raft with people who had very different backgrounds than your own? What are some things you learned as part of that tightly-knit group working together?*

Chapter Three:

Then There Were Three!

*H*aving a child was the most exciting and grueling event of my life up to that moment. Being pregnant in Korea, I did not have family close by to share in the anticipation, but I took excellent care of my health and stayed physically active, which included swimming at an indoor pool at Seoul Union Club downtown until I was nine months pregnant. Being responsible for another life was a deeply spiritual experience and a huge responsibility. It was a dying to selfishness, a loss of control of my own life, as well as a miracle of God's creativity. Since I had no prior childbirth experience, I welcomed the opportunity to work with an American midwife, a daughter of Baptist missionaries who had been educated in North Carolina. I never saw a Korean doctor, although Rebekah was delivered in a hospital where doctors were on call if needed. The midwife educated me about natural childbirth, coached me through my pregnancy and allowed me to labor in her home until it was time to deliver, since we did not have a car of our own and David felt safer in our midwife's home than on the seminary campus.

Since Rebekah arrived three weeks after her due date, my mother was present in time to be a full participant in the labor and delivery process. We made our way leisurely to the hospital when the midwife felt it was time. My mother and David took turns putting pressure on my back since I was experiencing "back labor" until it was time for me to push and Rebekah made her entrance. Rebekah Ann Hudson, our first daughter, arrived a little after 8:00 p.m. on May 10, 1985, after a long labor with no medication and no complications. Rebekah's appearance was a moment of joy unrivaled by any other in my whole life. David's words, "She's so beautiful!" reflected my feelings of intimate ecstasy. It was a long, brutal labor, but giving birth to another human being was an embodiment of grace, like I had never imagined. The joy on David's face, my mother's delight at being present, and my awe that God had created a living human being within my own body is difficult to capture in words. Holding Rebekah in my arms and being able to nurse her immediately helped me imagine how much God loves all of us and wants to nurture us. I may have been the vessel for Rebekah's arrival, but she is God's child first! No doubt God feels this deep connection to all of creation, which God has birthed!

I did not know enough to be concerned when we were standing outside the hospital at ten o'clock that same evening, only two hours after Rebekah's birth. We hailed a taxi back to the seminary from the hospital's parking lot! My mother kept her anxiety to herself but shared later with me how scary it was for her that we were transporting our newborn baby in a taxi at night across a crowded city like Seoul.

Rebekah was the only baby on the seminary campus, so she became quite a star! The Korean people all said the same thing about her: "Nun zup jom bah!" which is Korean for, "Look at those eyelashes!" The international church leaders were all studying without their families present, even though most had wives and children waiting for them in their home countries. Rebekah became everyone's baby. Hope, a pastor's daughter from the Philippines, and Beng Seng, from Malaysia, were Rebekah's closest "auntie" and "uncle." They married a few years later. Rebekah called Hope, "Ho-pe," with two syllables and would reach her arms out to be held by her.

There was never a shortage of people who wanted to hold and pay attention to Rebekah. She was also easy and attentive. Once she could sit up, she was content to sit and smile through many Bible studies and worship services without disrupting any of them. She grew up riding in my backpack as we rode buses, metros and taxis. When she was introduced to car seats in America at age two-and-a-half, it took a while for her to adjust to such confinement!

One memory of our weekly Bible studies with the international church leaders stands out in my mind. We were studying the Beatitudes in Luke's Gospel. I distinctly remember Hope speaking about the verse, "Blessed are you poor, for yours is the Kingdom of God."[5] In Matthew, Jesus' words are: "Blessed are the poor in spirit." Hope pointed out that western Christians tend to misinterpret Jesus' intention for blessing the poor, by "over-spiritualizing" the meaning of poverty, as humility of spirit. She said that Luke is more direct in showing the relationship between Jesus and the "literal poor." Having been raised in poverty in the home of a Christian minister, she was challenging us to

---

[5] Luke 6:20-23.

recognize the fact that the poor on the planet, literally, will inherit the Kingdom of Heaven, not the rich. When the rich young ruler asked Jesus what he should do to inherit the Kingdom of God, Jesus invited him to give away everything he had, but the man could not do it and went away disappointed.[6]

A high point of our time in Seoul took place in a small church near the seminary campus. Rebekah was baptized by Dr. Park Chang Whan, the president of the Presbyterian Theological Seminary. It was an honor and privilege to have Dr. Park, whom we deeply respected, baptize Rebekah. The entire service was in Korean until it was time for her baptism, when Dr. Park spoke in English, saying: "Rebekah, I baptize you in the name of the Father, and of the Son, and of the Holy Spirit. Amen." It was a moving moment for our family of three!

Both sets of Rebekah's grandparents made their way to Seoul to see her. My mom and dad came for the Asian Games in 1986 when Rebekah was one year old. It was my dad's first overseas adventure. The enticement of seeing his granddaughter and also watching the Asian Games, which were hosted in the same venues that would be used for the Olympics in 1988, provided the motivation and incentive for dad to ask mom to call the travel agent for his first trip outside of the United States! David's parents were on a China tour and added a personal extension to South Korea.

Although we left Seoul when Rebekah was two-anda-half-years-old, her love for rice, kiem and bulgogi has never abated. "Miya kuk," or seaweed soup, was

---

[6] Matthew 19:16-30, Mark 10:17-31, Luke 18:18-30.

the go-to healthy food for every mother after childbirth. Min Hee Yun, the secretary to the president of the seminary, who was my mentor for cooking Korean food from scratch, stocked me with lots of iron-rich seaweed soup at the time of Rebekah's birth. David and I extended an extra year to our missionary term in Seoul, but when I was seven-and-a-half months pregnant a second time, we returned to the United States to speak in our supporting churches.

Questions for Reflection:

> ➤ *When have you experienced an "embodiment" of God's grace in your life? Who was present with you during that experience?*

> ➤ *Is there a passage in the Bible (or other holy Scripture) that has always been special or important for you? Please share what it is and how it has shaped your life.*

Chapter Four:

Then There Were Four!

The next phase of my life was joyous and arduous. We moved from Korea back to the United States shortly before our second daughter, Rachel Leigh Hudson, was born. She was a challenging baby. She was born in a hospital, where I was attended by a doctor, rather than a midwife, simply because in Richmond, Virginia, mid-wives were not authorized to practice in hospitals and I did not want a home birth.

Rachel's entry was rather quick. We were watching television in our apartment until about eight or nine in the evening, while my labor pains began. My mom and dad stayed in the apartment to watch Rebekah; while, David and I headed off to the hospital. Rachel made her grand entrance at about 2:00 a.m. Thankfully, David and I knew the ropes of childbirth and did not need much help or attention from the doctor until it was time to push.

From the time of her birth, Rachel was eager to hit the road running, but did quite a bit of crying in the early days. When I could not calm her down, Nana, my mother, took over. David was out-of-town visiting churches in the first week of her life, so Pop-Pop, my father, found himself to be the man who could get Rachel to fall asleep. He was proud of that! My mother and I did not want to burst his bubble by telling him that by the time he held her, Rachel had already worn herself out. Nana was right, though. As soon as Rachel was old enough to sit and crawl, her crying days were over and her explorations began!

Rachel came down with chickenpox as a baby, so we had to cancel Rebekah's birthday party that year. Some of those early pictures of Rebekah, after Rachel was born, reflect that she was a bit shell-shocked by the changing rhythm of her life.

Our months in Richmond were hectic. Rachel was always in motion. We stayed in other peoples' homes when we were visiting our supporting churches. Since we were not in our own home, I often needed to rock her and walk her during the night to keep her content. While David and I spoke about our experiences as missionaries in Korea, Rachel was exposed to new church nurseries every Sunday morning. It would have been a much more trying time for me if we had not been welcomed and received on the Union Seminary Campus in Richmond, Virginia, where Rachel Weller, raised by missionary parents in Ethiopia, helped me find a doctor, had children for mine to play with, and showed me the ropes of living in Richmond.

We made the decision not to return to Korea, but to find employment in the United States. David's new job led us to Atlanta, Georgia, where he worked downtown at Friendship Force, a non-profit organization founded in 1980 by Wayne Smith, a former missionary, to promote intercultural relations, cultural diplomacy and friendship through homestays. David commuted to his work in the city from our apartment in the suburbs, so that I could use our car during the day.

The girls and I found a YMCA where I could participate in aerobics classes, Rebekah took swimming lessons, and there was child care for Rachel. Everyone took some deep breaths. Friends in our apartment complex introduced us to the recent invention of VHS tapes when they invited us to their home for dinner. With all the kids in front of their television watching movies, we had time for a few adult conversations. After a year's interlude in Atlanta where we celebrated Rachel's first birthday, we packed our bags and headed for David's first pastoral assignment in Troy, North Carolina.

Questions for Reflection:

> ➤ *Was there a place in your life that was similar to a quiet pool in between the rapids, where you could relax, jump off a few rocks, swim, splash, play and laugh together?*

> ➤ *What schedule or routine have you established for yourself and your family that keeps you healthy and balanced?*

Then There Were Five!

When we settled in Troy, North Carolina, there was never a dull moment. Shortly after our arrival, Hurricane Hugo passed through Charlotte. David's parents lost electricity for days. Everyone in our family, including my parents, converged on Troy, North Carolina, to celebrate this moment of God's anointing David for his first pastoral call. The loving church family in Troy welcomed and embraced us as their pastor and their pastor's family. They welcomed me as the pastor's wife and as a Christian educator, honoring me with an Honorary Life Membership in Presbyterian Women, which took me by complete surprise since that honor was often reserved for women who had been serving for decades.

We poured our love into that congregation and they poured their love into us. David and I both taught Sunday school. I saw a side of David that delighted me. He volunteered to teach the pre-school class, while I taught the older children. When I observed his teaching, I loved his spontaneous way of getting the kids' attention, which was not suggested by any particular curriculum. The preschoolers were captivated by his energy. When it was time to gather for the lesson, David took a small pillow and invited the kids to pound on the pillow with him as fast as they could and then slowly come to a stop. From that point forward, he had them in the palm of his hand.

I directed Vacation Bible School, assisted with Family Night Suppers, and served wherever else I was needed. Troy is where both Rebekah and Rachel began their education. In the middle of those settled years, we welcomed the birth of Mary Elizabeth Hudson in 1991. She is named after my mother. I had always promised my mom I would name a daughter after her, so God gave me one more chance to make good on that promise. Whew!

My parents were present when Mary was born. A friend of mine had given me information about a birthing center in High Point, North Carolina, where it was possible to experience a "water birth." Needless to say, I thought that sounded like a wonderful way to bring a child into the world. Mary arrived several weeks late, just like Rebekah and Rachel. After being in labor one night, I aroused the family and all of us went to High Point together, only to be told by the midwife that I was not dilated enough and needed to go back home and wait. Since High Point was about an hour from Troy, mom and I stayed in High Point to walk and wait, while David, Dad and the rest of the family went back to Troy. No sooner had they arrived home than my labor pains picked up speed and intensity. We called David and Rebekah to come back to High Point as soon as they could. Pop-Pop and Rachel stayed home.

I asked to labor for a while in the bathtub, but as the contractions became more intense, the confinement of the tub was too restrictive of my movement, so I asked for help to get back to the bed. David and Rebekah arrived just in time to be present for Mary's grand entrance to our family. After getting back to the bed, the midwife encouraged me to push. When Mary's head presented itself, I exhaled, relaxed, and had to be encouraged to continue pushing. In a few minutes, Mary was in my arms. As we had done with Rebekah, we made our way back to Troy a few hours after Mary's birth, as soon as the midwife had an opportunity to check her vital signs, make sure she was nursing happily, and there were no other concerns.

Pop-Pop and Rachel welcomed us home that evening. In those early days, Pop-Pop was nervous about the way Rachel energetically rocked Mary's cradle. Rachel was three when Mary was born. Not long afterwards Rachel was enrolled in the Montgomery Community College preschool program. She and both of her grandfathers loved to joke about the fact that Rachel attended college before she went to kindergarten!

One thing I have never forgotten is what I learned from Rachel while we said our nightly prayers when she was about four years old. We would pray for everyone we knew and loved: grandparents, aunts, uncles, cousins and immediate family. However, Rachel always concluded her prayer by saying, "And, thank you, God, for me." I loved that she took the time to pray for herself. I had to learn that lesson much later in my own life. Rachel would giggle and had an adorable smile on her face when she finished.

Our years in Troy were idyllic in many ways. It was a great place for David to hunt and fish, with plenty of space to care for his hunting dogs. I developed good friendships that have lasted through today. The girls had many friends as well. One summer after Mary was born, I taught swimming lessons with Laura Gingerich to our children and other children in the congregation, using the backyard swimming pool of some church members who worked and were not at home during the day. By babysitting their children, we earned rights to their pool all summer and gave out certificates to all the children for learning to swim. The Gingerichs lived on a farm outside of Troy and often invited us to their home for hikes, rides on their pony, and hours of fun.

Questions for Reflection:

> ➤ *Putting down roots in a small town when our daughters were young gave all of us a chance to breathe, play, and develop strong friendships. Can you describe a quiet pool of rest and refreshment in your life?*

> ➤ *Are there family rituals or traditions that continue to bring joy to your family and keep you connected even now?*

Chapter Six:

Summer Breaks: Pittsburgh, PA, 1989-1995

During those years of ministry, it was always a joy to go to my parents' home in Pittsburgh. Mom and Dad waited eagerly for us to share our children and stories with them. The Fourth of July was the best holiday for pastors to travel, so we got in the habit of attending the Fourth of July festivities in Mt. Lebanon Park. My dad would always negotiate some free passes to the outdoor public pool, which he would collect all summer and proudly offer us. The public pool, where I had spent most of my summer afternoons growing up, had been renovated and now had water slides with one that curved and dropped down like a spiral, and one that was a short dark tunnel that dropped the person into deep water. My dad loved challenging the girls on the spiral slide to see who could smack their bottoms at just the right time to make the greatest splash on the way down the slide. My dad could make anything into a lively competition!

Sandcastle Water Park was also an annual outing we could not miss. The park is located on the banks of the Monongahela River near the heart of Pittsburgh. It features fifteen waterslides, a wave pool, a lazy river and two children's play areas. Pop-Pop loved to take the girls to the top of the highest, fastest waterslide. Mary was slightly shorter than the required height one year, but Pop-Pop talked the lifeguard into letting her go down the slide. When the lifeguards changed shift, however, Pop-Pop's powers of persuasion did not suffice and Mary had to walk back down the steps by herself, feeling a bit embarrassed. Pop-Pop was someone who always challenged people to push their limits, overcome their fears, and "go for the gold!"

Questions for Reflection:

➢ *Most of our Hudson vacations meant visiting our families in Pittsburgh and Charlotte. Where have you and your family had fun together?*

➢ *What types of recreation, hobbies or other activities have given you joy?*

Chapter Seven:

Letting Go and Letting God: Lahore, Pakistan 1995-1997

While we lived in Troy, the thought of doing mission work was always percolating under the surface of our minds. We looked into a position that would have been a pioneering role in Uzbekistan, a former territory in the Soviet Union; however, that position was not offered to us. Then one day, David asked me: "Would you consider going to Pakistan?" Before I knew it, airline tickets were in the mail for us to Louisville, Kentucky, for an interview at the Presbyterian Church (USA) headquarters. Our trip to Louisville turned out to be not an opportunity to vote the position up or down, but rather an initiation into a job that I never felt we had officially accepted. We were hired.

The call to Pakistan was a little unnerving to me with three daughters, ages four, seven and ten. This new chapter of our lives was an intense journey for me to empower myself and my daughters for another challenging environment, without close friends and family as a network of support. This time I felt like a mother hen with three chicks following behind her into a threatening environment. Right before we left for Pakistan, I began to feel a call to ministry myself and wondered how on earth God would bring it to fruition. While in

Pakistan, I read Carol Gilligan's book, *In a Different Voice,*[7] and began to discern how my voice was different from David's and how important it was for me to honor my own needs and express them more directly.

As we prepared for the journey to Pakistan, a new season of letting go and letting God had begun. When I informed my dad of our plans, he thought I was crazy and nearly shouted at me over the telephone: "What about the girls?" I answered, "David and I think it will be good for the girls to have an overseas experience during their childhood." Letting go meant saying goodbye to people we loved. We knew that we better not tell Rachel about this new plan until we were ready for everyone to hear about it. Sure enough, when we broke the news, she helped us share it with everyone in our neighborhood. One person informed me that if she were one of my daughters, she would be angry. Step one of making this transition for our family required that we let go of other peoples' expectations.

Our girls were young enough to buy into the adventure. I particularly remember the lesson we learned when I asked each of them to pack one special trunk with their prized possessions to leave behind in Pittsburgh. All the rest of the toys, like the Fisher-Price kitchen set, had to be given away to a yard sale or friends. More letting go. We each would bring one big suitcase of clothes to Lahore.

The toughest and most shocking letting go experience was when everyone we loved gathered at the airport in Charlotte, North Carolina, to say goodbye. Rachel, age seven, was energized by all the company and attention

---

[7] Gilligan, Carol, *In a Different Voice,* Cambridge, MA: *Harvard University Press* 1982.

we were receiving from grandparents, aunts, uncles and cousins. When we boarded the plane, the truth began to sink in that she probably would not see those same people for years. Her laughter turned quickly to tears. We huddled together on the airplane to comfort her, for though Rachel was the most expressive of her feelings, this was a challenging moment for all of us.

Once we arrived in Lahore airport, I went into the bathroom and changed into my new clothes, which David had secured for me, so that I would not be wearing western apparel when our church partners in Lahore picked us up. I later discovered that Pakistani women could wear more colorful materials and styles than the clothes David first gave me. In fact, most women had their clothing made by tailors in the market, which I learned to do as well. Letting go introduced me to a whole new custom-made wardrobe!

Our initial housing was in the Presbyterian Guest House near the train station at the congested center of Lahore. The Presbyterian Church of Pakistan's office was right next door, so the Guest House was conveniently located for public transportation. The five of us moved into one room at the Guest House with three single "char-pai" (woven beds) to share. There was also a large kitchen. But, the rooms had separate air conditioners so that when we had to go into the hallways the heat was almost unbearable.

I decided we needed to make this fun, so I wrote the numbers one through five on small slips of paper and we put them in a bowl to pick from each night. The persons who drew numbers one through four would each have to share a "char-pai," and whoever picked number five would have a whole "char-pai" for herself/himself.

Every night we picked new numbers. We learned as the nights passed that whichever number I picked, even if it was number five, little Mary always found her way onto my "char-pai" to keep me company. When I shared this memory with Rebekah, she remembers it differently. She says Mary would often fall asleep on the number five "char-pai," before the rest of us went to bed. Of course, mom and dad did not want to awaken a sleeping child, whereas Rebekah would have been willing to awaken her in a heartbeat!

Crossing the street in front of the guesthouse was daunting because there were too many lanes of traffic to count. All lanes went one direction around the train station, but no one stayed in a lane. David and I would hold hands and asked all the girls to hold onto us tightly, as we moved "en masse" across the street, dodging taxis, cars, rickshaws, motorcycles and an occasional camel.

Many months later, when we found housing near the Lahore American School, an Assembly of God mission co-worker was trying to sell his family's furniture and possessions. For a reasonable price, God provided our family exactly what we needed in the way of furniture, which included a complete set of hardback Nancy Drew mystery books for the girls. All the furniture looked better than what we had left behind. Letting go and letting God turned out not to be so bad after all.

Being the youngest child can be an advantage. When we finally moved into our rental house near the school, Mary, age four, was the only one who had the opportunity (and lack of fear) to climb the ladder over the wall in our yard to play with the girls next door. She shared her Barbie dolls with them and played in their home because she did not see a difference between herself and the girls who lived there. We learned later that many girls in Pakistan were not given the opportunity to go to school because, if families had limited funds, they only educated their sons. If I remember correctly, the girls that lived next door did not attend school but freely welcomed their American next-door neighbor to play with them.

Once David began working, I would ride with the girls in a rickshaw – a three-wheeled vehicle propelled by liquid propane gas. The driver sat in front and the four of us girls were packed like sardines on a seat that would be comfortable for two adults. I remember riding with the girls and looking out around me at the bustling city of Lahore, knowing that not a single person on the planet knew where we were or could help us if anything happened. Eventually, David and I bought a car and a motorcycle. He rode all three girls on the back of his motorcycle to school each morning, which they thought was awesome.

One day I was bringing the girls home from a birthday party. At a busy red light in the middle of Lahore, my car would not start! A young man on a motorcycle offered to assist me and parked his motorcycle at the side of the road. We knocked on someone's door to use their phone. This was way before the era of cell phones. I called David for advice. David insisted the car had plenty of water, so the motorcycle driver got the car started and drove us home. When we arrived safely, after stopping to put water in the engine anyway, David realized there was a leak in the water hose after all. Our Good Samaritan had safely brought our family home, but the engine was melted and needed to be rebuilt.

Another time I was driving the car by myself and pulled over to a fruit stand by the side of the road.

Most Pakistani women did not drive in those days. Unfortunately, I did not see a deep hole on the side of the road. One front tire sank into the hole, while the rest of the car was lifted into the air. I barely had time to feel fear before several men pulled over in their cars, lifted my car out of the hole and made it level. Without my even having time to say thank you, the men were gone! I felt respected and protected by a few more Muslim Good Samaritans. Letting go of stereotypes is liberating.

During our first year as Mission Specialists in Lahore, Pakistan, Benazir Bhutto, the first female Muslim Prime Minister of any country, was dismissed from power unexpectedly. Her father had been the first democratically elected president in Pakistan; however, the young democracy never had a peaceful transition of power. Our daughters' school closed down that day for fear of violence in reaction to her removal. Later Bhutto went into exile. In 2007 she was violently murdered during a Homecoming Parade honoring her return to the country.

When our Supervisor from the Presbyterian Church, Dr. Victor Makari, came to visit us that year, I confided in him that I felt called to ordination, after living and serving in a country where women did not have that freedom. I remember speaking at a Women's Conference at Gujranwala Seminary. A male minister had to give the opening prayer to begin the conference, rather than a woman, even though it was a women's conference. In churches on Sunday mornings, women sat on one side and men sat on the other. I was careful to cover my head in church out of respect for all of the women in the sanctuary.

In the Christian Education classes I taught at the seminary, there were a few female students who often seemed to be the brightest and most promising in the class. On a few occasions, when I was unable to travel from Lahore to Gujranwala, I delegated my teaching to Mrs. Nosheen Khan, an educator in the class, to be my substitute teacher. At that time in the Presbyterian Church of Pakistan, the door was closed to her ordination. My sense of call to ordination grew stronger in a culture where women did not have that freedom. Dr. Makari confidently responded to my desire, saying, "Sue, the Presbyterian Church would be blessed to have you as a Minister of Word and Sacrament." I wasn't sure how that would fit with my calling to be serving as a Mission Co-worker in Pakistan, but his affirmation and support empowered me to move forward.

As it turned out, I returned to the United States each summer to do coursework and take ordination exams, rather than retreating to the cooler hills of Pakistan with other missionary wives. The first summer I took an eight-week concentrated Hebrew class at Princeton and had to leave after six weeks so that I could get our daughters back to Lahore for their first day of school. In the Hebrew final exam, which I had to take two weeks before the class ended, I had to translate a passage from Hebrew into English, but it was not a familiar passage for me. Ironically, the passage was one in which Moses' father-in-law was urging him to delegate some of the work he was doing to others so that he would not get burned out as the leader of God's people. That's not a common Sunday school text, but I have come to appreciate it in a whole new way after thirty-nine years of mission and ministry!

I had whined and worried about the grade I would get on the test the whole way back to Pittsburgh with my parents. All three girls were still in Charlotte with David's parents. When I received an A- for my final grade, my dad declared he would never again listen to my whining about how hard a test was.

The girls enjoyed spending three weeks with each set of grandparents during that first summer. When it came time to return to Pakistan, we all had a big suitcase, so it took my dad two trips to the Pittsburgh airport to get us and all of our baggage there. A huge thunderstorm caused our flight to be canceled in Pittsburgh, which caused us to miss our connection in New York for Pakistan. We were flying on Kuwaiti Airlines, but that flight only departed once a week, so we had to change our tickets to Pakistani Airlines.

My dad negotiated with some airport officials to keep our rain-soaked suitcases in a locked room so that he would not have to take them all home again and then back to the airport the next morning. It seemed that every single leg of our journey had a glitch. Once we finally arrived in London, we had a twelve-hour wait for our flight to Lahore. We sat in Heathrow Airport all day, sharing one Sprite with four straws so that we could keep a table in one of the restaurants, while I taught the girls how to play bridge to pass the time.

When it was time to board our plane, after our twelve-hour wait, our flight was canceled because of a broken windshield on the plane. All of the passengers were transported to a hotel in London for the night. Rebekah remembers that dinner was served in two different lines. The regular hotel guests were served steak and fries while the passengers from the canceled flight were served soup and crusty bread. Rebekah's memory for details is amazing!

The next morning, we retraced our steps back to Heathrow airport for one more try at getting a flight to Lahore. The girls and I were definitely dragging. We finally arrived late at night the next day, with the girls having missed their first day of school. As we walked into the airport when the plane landed in Lahore, the heat and pollution at midnight made it difficult for us to breathe. David picked us up in a church van for another year of life in Lahore.

Rebekah was in sixth grade that year and I was so proud of her when she aced her test on Islam. Her immersion into a predominantly Muslim country led to a deeper understanding of that faith, and how it differs from Christianity, which was not diluted with Santa Claus stories during those years overseas. Our Christmas tree was a large potted plant, with a few sticks as branches. In Lahore, they celebrated Jesus' and Mohammad's birthdays on the same day. The girls had every Friday off school for the holy day of Islam and went to school on Sundays.

The second year in Lahore brought me an unexpected new responsibility. I became the Acting Director of the Educational Promotion Society, when the Director was accused of sexual misconduct. The Bishop of Lahore for the Church of Pakistan asked me to step in as an interim director. I was already serving on the Board of Directors for the non-profit organization that funneled money from Kindernothilfe (KNS) in Germany to impoverished children in Pakistan. It was awkward being a female director over an all-male staff. Although I could not speak Urdu fluently, I did the best I could.

How was I challenged spiritually in Pakistan? The book, *Things Will Be Different for My Daughter: A Practical*

Guide to Building Her Self-Esteem and Self-Reliance,[8] by Mindy Bingham and Sandy Stryker, became my life raft during those years. As I took the "Self-Test" at the beginning of the book, I found my growing edge to be in the area of assertiveness. That was a spiritual muscle I needed to develop. Looking back, living in Pakistan with three daughters was indeed, "Assertiveness Boot Camp," with God as my trainer. I practiced being a leader in three areas as a seminary professor, an interim director of a non-profit, and someone who assisted a gifted principal as she was establishing a Christian Girls' School called Kinnaird Academy.

It became a joke in our family during those years that mom/Sue had difficulty "saying no." The best example of this was when a strong German woman wanted to give me some of her daughter's used clothing. She had a well-made German wool coat for winter. She wanted $50 for it. In order to avoid seeing her, I would depart by different school gates, because it was too hard for me to articulate: "I don't want your daughter's coat." Saying "no" to people is a skill for which I have needed remedial training! David said he would be happy to tell the lady "NO!" We weren't going to spend $50 on the coat, even if it was made in Germany. I didn't want to hurt the woman's feelings. David got the job done. Our family's favorite store for clothes in Pittsburgh, was the Red, White and Blue, a Consignment Store, where we found high-quality clothes at a much cheaper price!

David's work in Lahore focused primarily on the Presbyterian Church's relationship with Forman

---

[8] *Things will be Different for My Daughter: A Practical Guide to Building Her Self-Esteem and Self-Reliance*, Mindy Bingham and Sandy Stryker, (New York, NY: Penguin Books), 1995.

Christian College and with the Presbyterian Church of Pakistan's Education Board, which oversaw Christian schools and hostels throughout the country. Forman Christian College was founded in 1864 by Dr. Charles W. Forman, a Presbyterian missionary from the United States. Forman stressed the rejection of rote learning and introduced the highest standards of modern learning and critical thinking. Originally known as the Lahore Mission College, the school was dedicated to collegiality and compassion, in keeping with the college motto, "By Love Serve One Another." Dr. Forman originally founded the school to educate the sons of Hindu, Sikh and Muslim leaders in English and to have them encounter the message of the Christian Gospel in their daily life.

By the time of Forman's death in 1894, nearly nine-hundred students were attending the school. For many decades, Forman was one of the premier educational institutions on the subcontinent. It was there that the research of Nobel Laureate, Dr. Arthur Compton, culminated in his receiving the Nobel Prize for physics in 1927. Later, during the 1947 Partition of India, the college converted two hostels into a hospital for refugees, which birthed United Christian Hospital. Forman is known as "a model of interfaith harmony," where mutual tolerance, appreciation and forbearance characterize campus life.

Forman Christian College was nationalized by the Pakistani government in 1972 under the banner of "Islamic Socialism," and it remained under government control until 2003. This thirty-year period was one of remarkable decay and dissolution on the campus. However, the faith of the church in Pakistan never wavered. This jewel of Pakistan was prayed about by

Pakistani Christians for thirty years. People outside of Pakistan had little hope that the Islamic Republic of Pakistan would ever consider returning the school to an American Christian church.

In the middle of the 1990s, discussions began about the future of Forman Christian College, which was once like the Harvard or Yale of Asia. The school had been an ecumenical effort in the Punjab; however, the Presbyterian Church (USA) was the owner of the property. When David and I arrived on the scene in Lahore, David and others, who were advising him from the Presbyterian Church (USA), entered into negotiations with the government about the condition of the school. I remember David telling the story when we were sharing our missionary experiences, that this situation could be described like this: "Someone stole your car, then wrecked it, and now wants you to pay for the price of having it re-built and returned to operation."

Humor and diplomacy are two of David's gifts. When we arrived in Pakistan in 1995, it was clear that the Board of Forman Christian College was a non-functioning board and needed to be re-constituted. One of David's tasks as a mission co-worker was to contact all of the existing board members and ask them to resign. Some of the individuals being asked to resign would be invited to serve on the new board, but some would not. I remember David's relief when he came home one evening and told me the story of how he successfully, and with a good rapport, asked one particular individual who was particularly problematic, to resign. The man did as he was asked, and David continued to have a good relationship with that man, even though he was not invited back on the board.

The negotiation with the government of Pakistan was about their giving just compensation to the Presbyterian Church for the land, which was a very high-priced and valuable piece of land in the Gulberg neighborhood. The government made the decision not to provide compensation, but rather to return the property and the school to the Presbyterian Church (USA) in hopes that the church would bring the school back to its former level. The official return of the school happened in 2003 after we were no longer serving in Pakistan; however, David had the privilege of being part of that negotiation and seeing the answered prayers of Pakistani Christians and missionaries around the world. People of all faiths in Pakistan revere the educational and medical work of Christian schools and hospitals in their country.

Forman Christian College is now thriving and is the only four-year Liberal Arts baccalaureate program in the country. The university currently offers twenty-one bachelor's degrees, graduate studies with five master's degree programs, including degrees in Biotechnology, Chemistry and Applied Economics. There is also an MBA/Executive MBA program, and an Executive MA in Public Policy from the College's Center for Public Policy and Governance. Forman's faculty is one of the most highly educated in Pakistan. The climate of academic freedom makes the campus attractive to the best instructors, given the growing restrictions on speech and actions on most campuses. To God be the glory![9]

---

[9] The information about Forman Christian College's history was obtained from Rev. Samuel A. Schreiner III, who presently serves as the Executive Director of Friends of Forman Christian College. The history Sam shared with me was written by Mary-Linda Armacost.

It was a privilege to serve in Pakistan during the years of those answered prayers. As our second year in Pakistan was drawing to an end in the spring of 1997, I was planning to go back to the United States to take ordination exams. While preparing with the girls for that summer, I had a sense in my spirit that I would not be back for a third year in Pakistan. God was whispering within me that I was being led home for a reason. I loved working with Zeb Zaman, a strong Christian woman who, after a career as a principal in a government school, was charting off to establish a Christian private school for girls. I was privileged to work with her that year as she planned for the school's opening. I did not want to disappoint her! However, when I said goodbye to her at the beginning of the second summer, I explained: "If I felt this call to go home and ignored it, I would never forgive myself if something happened to my mother."

The girls and I moved in with my parents when school let out in Lahore at the end of May. My mother and dad loved their full-time grandparent role that summer while I worked on classes for ordination. At the time my mother's health was stable; however, she had lived through three heart bypass surgeries. Those were hectic months for me to finish up all of my studies and preparation for my ordination exams scheduled for September. We enrolled the girls in the same schools that I had attended that fall: Julia Ward Howe Elementary School, where Mary was in first grade and Rachel was in fourth grade. Rebekah entered Mellon Junior High School.

Looking back on those months, I realize that I took my mother for granted, allowing her to do all the cooking and childcare so that I was free to study and spent many hours at the seminary. At Howe Elementary, most of the students went home for lunch, just as I had done as a child. Mom loved making peanut butter and bacon sandwiches and bacon, lettuce and tomato sandwiches for the girls when they came home for lunch. My dad loved teasing them as he watched them walking to and from school together, staying about six feet apart the whole way.

One of my dad's priorities that fall was to plan a big party for his and my mom's fiftieth wedding anniversary in October 1997. Although I was busy, and slightly harried with the planning process, Mom kept telling Dad not to make a big fuss. But Dad was adamant that there would be a big celebration at Hugo's Restaurant with all of their college, church, and officiating friends, along with running buddies and Mom's closest girlfriends and their spouses. My brother and I organized some funny refereeing skits and family skits to entertain the guests with Rebekah, Rachel and Mary taking parts. Dad's stubborn determination to celebrate fifty years of marriage was one of the greatest memories we shared as a family.

Barely a month after their celebration, when I had just begun to apply for ministry positions in the United States, my mother was diagnosed with inoperable brain cancer. As Thanksgiving had approached, she was not feeling great. We shared Thanksgiving dinner with my dad's brother's family so that mom would not need to cook. The next week, my mom had been feeling intense muscle pain. Her doctor recommended an M.R.I., which gave us the terrible news about her cancer.

Mom often laid in the bathtub reading historical fiction novels. Shortly after her diagnosis, I sat down beside her and asked her to please forgive me for the spoiled child I had been since I returned from Pakistan.

I was often short with her and unappreciative of the way she was taking care of us. I could not have done it without her. She did not want me to apologize and said she was happy to do what she had been doing. I asked her to please forgive me so that I would be able to live with myself from that day forward. She offered me the gift of forgiveness right there on the bathroom floor. Her final regrets about knowing the end was near for her were these: "I wish I could live to see your brother in a more stable and happy place. And I wish I could live to see your daughters grow up. Otherwise, I am ready to meet the Lord."

After going on three job interviews, I was offered a job in Florida one week before my mother's diagnosis. It was an excruciating and bittersweet time in my life. I was studying pastoral care for those who are dying at the very same time I was living with my mother who was dying. My emotions were stretched to the limit. I went for pastoral care every week in order to bear the load I was carrying. From the time of my mother's diagnosis until her death was only seven weeks.

David returned from Pakistan during that seven-week period. Thanks be to God, we were there with our three children to surround Mom with love and care for the last seven weeks of her life. I did all of her Christmas shopping, pampering her as much as she would allow. I hosted a Christmas Eve Supper, to which my brother and his girlfriend were invited, so that all of us would be able to attend the Christmas Eve worship service together, nearly filling up a whole pew in the sanctuary.

David, the girls and I went down to Charlotte to spend a few days with his parents over the Christmas holidays since he had not seen his parents in two years.

Given mom's diagnosis, it was hard for me to be away. We returned to Pittsburgh to celebrate David's birthday. Mom had purchased pork roast and sauerkraut, one of David's favorites, before we arrived. But Mom did not have the strength to lift the food out of the refrigerator. I immediately took over and announced to the whole family that we all needed to pitch in and serve Mom. As it turned out, that was our last celebratory meal together as a family. It was an emotional time. Mom's pastor and friend, Dr. Larry Selig, came and anointed her with oil that same week and prayed for her healing. We savored every day from that moment forward.

In the few weeks that followed, Mom went to the hospital and did not come back home until she went on Hospice Care for her last ten days on this earth. I visited Mom in the hospital one Saturday morning. She was sitting up in a chair, drinking a cup of coffee, when we had our last conversation. She said, "If you could move up the date of your ordination and I could take one more chemo treatment, perhaps I could make it to the service." We laughed and talked and then mom laid down to take a rest. She slipped into a semi-comatose state as I was sitting beside her. I knew that nothing traumatic or painful transpired while I was there. She simply did not respond verbally, sit up, or get out of bed ever again.

Rachel had been making it a habit to give my mom "healing kisses" as she laid in bed, but at one point, before mom lost the ability to communicate, she asked me to tell Rachel they were "comfort kisses," so that her heart would not be broken when the inevitable happened. Mom passed away on January 20, 1998, at home in her hospital bed, with Dad and me by her side.

Although I had accepted a pastoral call to Trinity Presbyterian Church in Venice, Florida, I told them I could not guarantee a start date, because I needed to care for my mother. If they needed to move more quickly with someone else, I encouraged the church to do that. However, they waited for me and held the position open. It was ironic and deeply painful that I had to start my first call to ministry at the moment of my most profound grief. Four weeks after my mother's death, our family said goodbye to my father and moved to Florida for me to pursue that call, since David had resigned from the position we shared in Pakistan. The children were in first, fourth and seventh grades, and had to make another move in the middle of the school year. I was thrown out of my raft and felt caught in some hydraulic waves that kept flipping me round and round before I could catch my bearings and get back into my family's raft. I needed the help of our whole family to keep on functioning.

Questions for Reflection:

> ➤ *When did your raft get swamped and almost sink? In what ways did God help you through that experience?*

> ➤ *Reflect on a time in your life when you felt "nudged by God" and had to trust that nudge, even when your raft capsized, and everyone in the raft fell out?*

Chapter Eight:

Another New Beginning: Venice, Florida

*I*t was awkward timing. The new Associate Pastor for Family Ministries arrives a month after her mom's death, swamped in grief, but charged with bringing vitality and joyful energy to children, youth and parents in a church that was primarily filled with retired snowbirds from the North. There is a saying in Southwest Florida that grandparents retired to Sarasota while great-grandparents retired to Venice. The shops on the island closed at five o'clock every night.

David was following me on my career path for the first time in our marriage, right at the moment I would have loved to be following him so that I could take time to grieve. Thankfully, the Catholic Church on the island offered an eight-week Grief Support Group. I scheduled a visit with a parish nurse about starting up a grief support group at my church, but when she learned that my mother had died so recently, she recommended that I simply participate in a group for myself. I remember her words clearly: "You cannot lead one of these groups with such fresh grief. You need to attend one!" That was excellent advice. I was free to cry, be human, and tell my story at a church where I was not employed.

In the middle of Vacation Bible School that summer, which I was coordinating, I came home midweek and sat down on the floor and cried like a baby. Fortunately, it was in the middle of the Grief Support Group I was attending. My children put their arms around me and prayed for me that day. Mary, our youngest, looked at me tenderly and said, "Don't you think Nana would want you to be happy again?" That was a loving wake-up call from my mom's namesake. "Yes, honey. I know she does. It's just easier said than done. I will try to find my happiness again."

My service of ordination took place in Pittsburgh six months after my mother's death. It was a bittersweet moment. Mom's last words revealed her deep desire to be with me when I was ordained. I stopped at the cemetery on the way to church before the service to have a brief chat with her there. David's family and my family came for the service, as did many of my friends from the church where I grew up, surrounding me with their loving presence.

By Christmas, we were living in a new house and putting up decorations in Venice. One of my favorite door hangings was handmade in Korea by people with special needs. It spells J-O-Y! I put it directly on the glass door on the front of our house, but every time I came home, it was on the ground. I couldn't get the right adhesive that would hold it securely to the door. It became a symbol of that Christmas in my life. After re-enacting the Christmas story with all the children and families at the Christmas Eve Worship Service, I came home and found my "Joy Banner" on the ground, literally and figuratively.

My last worship service with my mom the year before had been Christmas Eve, with our whole extended family sitting on the pew together. Mom was still wearing her beloved high-heeled shoes, even though she had stumbled up our front porch steps when we got home that night. Grief washed over me that Christmas Eve, so I sobbed in my bedroom. That was our children's first Christmas in Venice.

I felt like a single parent in Venice as David took interim positions, first as a Pastor and later as the Executive Presbyter. The girls and I went to church together and participated in all of the children, youth and family activities. I loved preaching and loved the people at Trinity Presbyterian Church, but my heart longed for our family to be worshipping together again. We began to look for another call. My dream was for us to serve as co-pastors because it felt like I had been a single parent for too long. I knew that David and I shared the same core values in ministry and wanted our family to be worshipping in one place while our girls still lived at home. We circulated our resumes and received a call to become co-pastors at Bethesda Presbyterian Church in Aberdeen, North Carolina. Although they were looking for one pastor, Ann McNeill, a Commissioned Ruling Elder and Chairperson of the Pulpit Nominating Committee, asked the congregation to vote on the decision to take two instead of one, which they voted to do, dividing the salary between us.

Questions for Reflection:

➢ *When has an experience of grief or loss thrown you out of your boat?*

➢ *When has your "role" in life (mother/father/child/ grandparent/employee/caregiver) required you to suppress or over-ride your inner feelings or emotional needs simply to survive, because you were the person steering the boat?*

Chapter Nine:

Finding Family Roots

*A*lthough we had bought a house and intended to have a long and wonderful ministry in Florida, we let go of that dream. For our children, it was almost too much to take: another move! Rebekah gave us a "Certificate of Diagnosis for Obsessive-Compulsive Moving Disorder!" She has been the family comedian and entertainment coordinator ever since. Letting go of the sparkling promise of becoming settled in our new house, the children packed their bags. We never hung pictures on the walls in our house on Wordsworth Way.

William Wordsworth was one of my mother's favorite poets, so when we had purchased that house, I had felt her blessing. Rachel told me later it was the hardest move she ever had to make. I asked David to dig up the maple tree planted in our yard in memory of my mother. Then I made the trek from Florida to North Carolina by myself, with our three chickadees in our white mini-van. The girls and I cried as we drove up the road and said goodbye to our first house. David stayed behind to finish his employment and followed us a month later.

Our former friend from Troy, Laura Gingerich, met us after we settled into a small hotel room. She took us to Reservoir Park for a picnic and canoeing. What a delight to be reunited with her! She and her husband had moved to nearby Moore County during the years we were away. With Laura's help and David's blessing from Florida, I found a house to buy, which belonged to an older church member whose daughter lived down the street. We had already moved in before David showed up to see it for the first time. It was a beautiful home on a quiet street, but David was concerned about its proximity to a busy street behind us. He quickly set about the task of planting evergreens along the fence. That was eighteen years ago. Now the backyard of that house is completely hidden from the street. Somehow, I knew even then that it would not be our forever home.

The transition into our next ministry had its challenges, but it was my dream and desire for David and me to work together so that our family would not be divided. We have complementary styles of ministry. He is more the administrator with oversight of finances, building and grounds, along with the leadership of the governing bodies. My ministry skills gravitate towards Christian education, youth ministry, spiritual growth, Stephen Ministry and mission trips. David and I both shared in the preaching and pastoral care. Working with the Confirmation classes each year was one of my passions; I loved guiding young people in their faith formation. I also loved coordinating women's retreats and "Gifts of Women" worship services, where I had the opportunity to choreograph movement and liturgy, inviting women to exercise their gifts and leadership in innovative ways.

After the initial adjustments, our daughters found a spiritual home there and sunk roots in that community. Since our home had a fenced in back yard, Mary's wish for a puppy came true during our first

Christmas in Southern Pines. We welcomed Sandy, a golden retriever, into our family. Rachel's dream to continue riding horses was fulfilled when she became a working student at Fox Track Farm where Mel Wyatt taught riding lessons to young people and also ran summer camps with her "working students" as assistants. Rebekah was simply happy to settle down and finish high school in one location.

The girls were active in youth activities and worship leadership at Bethesda. Rebekah's "Senior Moment" during the Youth Service was a take-off from late-night comedy, as she shared with the congregation, "The Top Ten Things You Always Wanted to Know about Being a Minister's Kid." Most seniors share sentimental thoughts and memories, but Rebekah had everyone in stitches. Both Rachel and Mary were active in the youth group and were ordained as youth elders, while they were in high school. I remember Mary assisting me in choreographing a liturgical dance for the youth to implement during a Good Friday Service to accompany the song by Josh Groben, "You Raise Me Up." Mary was also the person the group raised up in the air as Josh's song played over the speaker system!

Questions for Reflection:

> ➢ *How do your passions and gifts connect with your community, your family of faith, or the world?*

> ➢ *Where have you and your family been able to grow roots and thrive?*

Stirring Up Our Passions

Our time at Bethesda was wonderful. One of my responsibilities was to help redevelop the youth ministry program. I utilized the resource, *Teaming Up: Shared Leadership in Youth Ministry*, by Ginny Ward Holderness, with Robert S. Hay.[10] Ginny also came to Bethesda and did an assessment of our ministry. The approach described in their book helps churches put less emphasis on a single Youth Director, who often cannot live up to peoples' expectations. The book shifts the focus towards recruiting parents and other adults within the church to work alongside the youth as part of the Youth Director's Team. The Team tries to discern God's vision and direction for their youth ministry, as well as the best ways to implement that ministry within their church and community. While accompanying our youth to Montreat Senior High and Middle School conferences every summer, I also volunteered to serve as a Small Group Leader, where youth could delve more deeply into the themes and content of the conferences.

When our youngest daughter, Mary, was fourteen, she approached me at one of those conferences and said she would like to travel back overseas to have a

---

[10] Ginny Ward Holderness with Robert S. Hay, *Teaming Up: Shared Leadership in Youth Ministry.* (Louisville, Kentucky: Westminster John Knox Press), 1997.

cross-cultural experience with her dad and me before she grew up. Mary had served earlier in the summer on the work crew for the Middle School Montreat Youth Conference in Clinton, South Carolina, at Presbyterian College. The theme for that conference was "Getting Out of the Boat," based on the story of Jesus inviting Peter to get out of the boat and walk on the water to meet him. She then attended the Senior High Montreat Youth Conference with the rest of our senior high youth. The theme for that event was "Crossing Borders." Both conferences urged the youth to take risks and get out of their comfort zones.

I was chaperoning the group and attended both conferences. Mary intentionally sat me down on a bench at Montreat with her request. I listened to her passion and held that desire, pondering it in my heart long after we got home. Later, I asked Mary if she still wanted to have an overseas experience, because once I shared that with Dad, it would set things in motion. Mary had planted the seed and it began to grow. I wanted to honor her desire. Asking David to consider mission service is like taking a match to a pile of dry twigs. We applied to World Mission for the Presbyterian Church (USA) and before long had received a call to serve as Regional Liaisons for South Asia.

Mary's sisters were out of high school and were moving on with their own lives, but when we accepted that call to mission, both were angry and felt abandoned. We broke the news to Rebekah and Rachel on Father's Day in 2006, a year before we would leave Bethesda. They were devastated and stunned by our decision. Rebekah had learning disabilities and ADD, so I had spent a lot of energy through her school years encouraging and supporting her. She was graduating from college and fully expected to move back home. Because she had not enjoyed living in Pakistan, she was adamant that she would not join us in India. (Years later, she did admit that her educational experience in Pakistan was excellent.)

Rebekah felt like the carpet had been pulled out from underneath her. She would be graduating from Queens University of Charlotte in the spring of 2007. She eventually moved into an apartment with three college friends but seemed on the verge of a break down before we left the country.

Rachel moved all of her belongings out of our home, when we were at missionary orientation in Toronto, Canada, and told us she could survive just fine without us. She was a rising senior in high school and would be attending college by the time we would be ready to leave. Deep in my core, I believed that what we were doing would be good for all five of us in different ways. Mary never wavered from her determination to make this move, but for her, it also meant saying goodbye to her sisters, all of her friends and supportive church family after her sophomore year of high school.

Talk about letting go. We sold our house and I preached my last sermon in March of 2007, which was a "Gifts of Women Service," with the women processing out of the sanctuary, as the congregation sang: "Guide My Feet." Our family moved temporarily into the home of one of our friends and church members, Laura Murdock, who was living in Hawaii with her family, while her husband served in the military there. Laura's home was on a lake in Whispering Pines. My other dear friend, Laura Gingerich, hosted a special meal for all of us, as it got closer to the time of our departure. My emotions overwhelmed me, as I realized that I would be leaving two of my children on one continent, while I departed to another. What was I thinking? How could I do this? Again, God whispered in my heart, and I believed that Rebekah would grow stronger and more independent, than if she moved home to live with us after graduating from college; and that Rachel might discover her need for us, or not. She was a highly independent young woman, who posted on Facebook after we left: "Homeless with a Minivan."

The day came to depart from Charlotte airport. Rebekah was with David's parents, as we walked through security and waved goodbye. David and I hugged and held each other and could not believe we were on our way to India. When I was on the phone with my sister-in-law, Robyn, while waiting to board our plane in New York, I got choked up and could not speak. She was going through a divorce and I was her closest confidante.

Mary would join us later in the summer after we secured housing in Delhi. She worked as a lifeguard at Camp Monroe and then attended the Presbyterian Youth Triennium, as a representative of our Presbytery's Youth Council, before joining us in India. Wheels up one more time. On our way to New Delhi, India. This was a terrifying moment, like jumping off a cliff into an unknown body of water.

Questions for Reflection:

> ➤ *When has God led you to let go of the people you love the most?*

> ➤ *Where is God calling you to use your gifts and talents right now? What sacrifices could it require of you as you follow God's leading?*

The Plunge

*M*y heart was fully engaged in this call to mission service, even though it felt counter-intuitive to be leaving my oldest two daughters, especially with their feelings of anger and abandonment. I wondered if I was crazy or negligent! However, when I had ended our service in Pakistan, I had a deep sense at that time that I would like to go back into a missionary role in the future when my own life was more settled. Being a role model for women in the developing world has always been very important to me. Selling our house and dismantling all of our worldly possessions was never easy. For the fourth time on our family's journey, we were letting go of familiarity and worldly security.

From that moment forward I focused on journaling my prayers to God, a practice which I have used all of my life, but the prayers dove deeper than ever before. They were my life-lines. I knew I had chosen to get out of the boat to follow Jesus, and the only way I was going to make it would be by keeping my eyes fixed on that purpose. We arrived in Delhi, India, during the hottest and most miserable season of the year, so that we could set up a home before school started. We spent two weeks living at the YMCA while we looked for an apartment. I developed a rash on my face from riding around in rickshaws in the heat of the afternoons to look for housing. I also needed to get some prescription sunglasses to shield my eyes from the bright sunlight of the afternoons. However, my spirit stayed strong most of the time and I wrote, prayed and leaned into my faith in God. There were a handful of moments I felt afraid and unsafe, but they were few and far between under the circumstances. Thanks be to God!

We received a warm welcome from our partners in the Church of North India (CNI), which is a united denomination from many different mission-sending churches: Baptist, Presbyterian, Methodist, and others. Since Christians are a small minority in India, the two churches of North and South India (CNI and CSI), offer a united witness of Christian solidarity in that country. David's role in that setting was to support our partner churches in all of South Asia, which included Bangladesh, India, Nepal, Pakistan and Sri Lanka. My primary job was to serve at St. Thomas School for Girls in Delhi, at the request of the Church of North India. The new principal, Mrs. Amos, was a Christian who invited me to teach "Values Education" to all of the secondary students, as well as offering a small Christian support group at the primary and secondary schools.

Living in India was both agony and ecstasy. A whole book could be written about the short time we lived there. My faith grew by leaps and bounds. The rich experiences of learning about the culture and being welcomed into the life of the Church of North India were many. I was invited to preach a number of times: to the bishops of the Church of North India at their annual meeting, at the Free Church, Parliament Street in New Delhi, and other places around the country. Another enriching experience was writing monthly devotions for the *North India Church Review*, an English-medium publication produced by the Church of North India. The Editor-in-Chief, Sushma Ramswami, became a close friend while we lived there.

Getting to know the Young Adult Volunteers from the Presbyterian Church (USA) was also a high point. They were assigned to work with a supervisor, Rev. Thomas John, in the Church of South India, but came to Delhi on some of their vacations and stayed in our apartment where we could introduce them to places in Delhi. The Mar Thoma churches of South India trace their roots back to the Apostle Thomas, who traveled to the subcontinent and birthed the first Christian communities there, long before foreign missionaries arrived.

It was a joy to work with Mrs. Amos at St. Thomas School, along with the other teachers and students. I thought it was amusing that I was invited to teach Values Education when most schools in the United States have dropped such studies. If we had been able to remain in India longer, the goal was for me to create a curriculum for kindergarten through twelfth grades.

We enjoyed worshipping at the Free Church, Parliament Street, which we considered our home church, while we lived there. We became close friends with a special education teacher at St. Thomas School, Shanti Devadas, whose husband was the manager/ director of the YMCA and Guest House in Delhi, where we lived when we arrived there. Shanti invited Mary and me to sing in a Christmas Choir. We rehearsed for weeks before the performance. There were participants from churches all over the city, which allowed us to meet some amazing people.

Since Rebekah and Rachel planned to join us that first Christmas, I decided we needed to do something fun and exotic. I booked a high-class tent at a Camel Camp in Rajasthan. I wanted to show our children that missionaries and pastors do know how to have fun every once in a while! We traveled on trains to Rajasthan and visited museums as well as Camel Camp. The night in Camel Camp was everything I hoped it would be: a big bonfire, singing and dancing long into the night! The next day we trekked on camels through the desert. It was delightful to do something so far off the grid.

Our life was just beginning in New Delhi and we loved it. David made several trips to Pakistan and by the end of our first year, the government required that we leave for the summer and re-apply for employment visas the next year. We temporarily moved in with David's family in Charlotte, North Carolina, for the summer, eagerly awaiting our new employment visas. As it got closer and closer to Mary's senior year at the American Embassy School in New Delhi, we were all anxious about the future. Things weren't looking good for our return, but no one at the Indian Embassy said why or what was causing the delay of our visas.

I began to entertain the idea that we needed to let Mary go back to India on her own, and perhaps move in with her volleyball coach's family. They lived on the campus of the American Embassy School and had a daughter Mary's age. Mary came to me dejectedly one day and said: "I'm sure you won't let me go back and stay with the Anderson family." To her surprise, I said that I had, in fact, been thinking she should. In no time, the Indian government renewed her student visa, but not our employment visas. I put Mary on the plane to Delhi by herself. Being left behind was not nearly as exciting as being the one to chart a new course. I missed Mary tremendously and began running every day to give myself a sense of purpose.

Having sold our home the year before and ventured off with God, I was feeling abandoned and angry. Run, Sue, run. And so, I did. David was eventually hired by the Presbyterian Church to serve as the new Asia Coordinator after our former boss, Rev. Insik Kim, retired. It was beginning to look like we were not going back to India, but I was determined to keep trying so that I could return to our apartment in Delhi and to our daughter for her senior year of high school. In the meantime, we had to pack our bags and head to Louisville, Kentucky, the headquarters of the Presbyterian Church (USA).

Questions for Reflection:

> ➤ *I felt like I was in a raft by myself, running a Class IV rapids, abandoned by God, who was supposed to be the guide in my raft. When have you felt abandoned in your life?*

> ➤ *Describe a time when you have felt alone, invisible or unheard?*

Where is Home?

*F*ast forward to Christmas 2008: I loaded a sixteen-foot truck with belongings that we had given away to go to India in the summer of 2007. I headed from Charlotte, North Carolina to Louisville, Kentucky to try and set up a home for our three daughters and my father where we could share Christmas together. It was one or two weeks before Christmas. David was the new area coordinator of Asia for the Presbyterian Church (USA) and had no time off to make the trip. David's brothers and Rebekah helped me load up our things by collecting furniture that we had given away a year earlier. Mary was still in India. Rachel was at Westminster College, finishing up her fall semester. David unloaded the truck by himself in the dark when I finally arrived in Louisville. I was utterly exhausted, but he could not wait until the next day to unpack. A home was created. Everyone arrived.

One of our holiday outings was to visit the Museum at Churchill Downs, home of the Kentucky Derby, ten minutes from our apartment. We walked into the Museum and stopped at the Visitor's Table. A young woman asked: "So, where's home? Where are you from?"

Stop action! That was a moment frozen in time. The young woman had asked me a traumatic question. Dad is from Pittsburgh. David and I had sold our family home in Southern Pines while our furnished apartment in Delhi was unoccupied. Mary lived with another family on the school campus. During the previous summer, Rachel had moved in with her horseback riding coach. Rebekah lived with a college friend in Charlotte and was doing her best to become financially independent. This two-bedroom apartment in Louisville had not earned the right to be called home yet.

Like the children's storybook about a lost bird, called: *"Are You My Mother?"* by P.D. Eastman[11], the young woman's question struck a raw nerve in me. "Where is home? Where are we from?" That was the Christmas we all laid around on the floor and over-dosed on whole seasons of "Burn Notice" on televi-sion together. No one was preaching or coordinating worship services that Christmas. We were on an in-house-family-camp-out in Louisville, which did not feel like home to any of us. For me, home was having Rebekah, Rachel, Mary, David, Sue and Ray under the same roof: cooking, eating, cleaning up, watching television, laughing and going to Christmas church services together. We were stacked like sardines on couches and blow-up mattresses.

"Home is where your journey begins" is a well-known expression, but what if you don't know where home is? Unlike my children, I did know where home was for the first eighteen years of my life. I grew up on a street called Quest-end Avenue, but the quest was far from over! As a child, I had been envious of people who moved to different places and met new people. I hun-gered for adventure. Does God have a sense of humor,

---

[11] Eastman, P.D., *Are You My Mother?* (New York, NY: Penguin Random House LLC), 1960.

or what? Twenty-eight years after our honeymoon in Seoul, Korea, I was spinning in circles and grateful to have landed, even briefly, in a place where we could experience Christmas together as a family.

Questions for Reflection:

> ➢ *What qualifies as home for you?*

> ➢ *When have you felt homeless or lost at sea?*

Chapter Thirteen

Unemployed and Kneading Grace

After we arrived in Louisville, months went by without anyone from our church headquarters checking in on me. I began the Doctor of Ministry degree to find my tribe and process my experiences. A fellow student, concentrating in the counseling track, reached out to me and listened to my story of being displaced and separated from my daughter. He was a Catholic of Hispanic lineage and wondered why Presbyterians only had two categories for people like me: pastors and missionaries. What about people who minister to people on the street? He said, "Haven't you seen all of the Hispanic people here in Louisville, who have no one to care for them?" I honestly had not noticed, but through my brother in Christ, Adam Ruiz, I came to know an invisible population that functioned under the radar, many undocumented, who were doing jobs other Americans did not want to do and sending money home to their families.

Adam said, "Sue, you have a pastor's heart."

I replied, "I don't speak Spanish!"

His follow-up to that was: "I do." So, in partnership with Adam, I spent time with many Hispanic workers and professional people. I also met one young man who had been victimized by human trafficking. He was working at an Indian Restaurant three doors away from the Presbyterian Church where I worshipped and became my "Spanish tutor."

How did I deal with my simmering anger and sense of abandonment by the church I loved and served? I eventually did call the Executive Director of the Presbyterian Church and asked her if I could meet her confidentially. She invited me to her home. I told her how I had felt marginalized by our church, since all those who hired me and sent me to serve in India had made no effort to follow up with me or provide pastoral care when we could not go back. I asked her how she would feel in my shoes. She wondered if I still wanted to have a conversation with my so-called "team" at the headquarters. I replied that I'd be lying if I said no. The next day I received a call from my "team" and met with them for two hours, where I shared how I felt marginalized as a woman and neglected as their missionary. They listened, admitted their neglect, and two of the three apologized to me, for which I am grateful.

Questions for Reflection:

> ➢ *Describe a time in your life when you have felt angry, misunderstood, neglected or unjustly treated by people you respected greatly?*

> ➢ *Who has shown up in your life, at just the right time, when you needed them, as an "angel in disguise"?*

My India Bucket List

*A*s Mary's senior year of high school continued, I communicated with various Indian Embassies in the United States and was able to secure a tourist visa from the Embassy in Houston, Texas, which allowed me to return to India in February 2009. I went back to sell or disperse our belongings from the apartment we had rented there, and to accompany Mary for the remainder of her senior year of high school. The very day my visa arrived in the mail, I called my close friend, Laura Gingerich, and asked her if she would like to accompany me to India. She agreed without even taking a breath. Laura loves to travel and is a photographer, who skillfully documents her travel experiences. We booked our flight and headed to New Delhi, where I fully intended to see, do and experience everything that was on my "India Bucket List," before I came home again.

Later in the spring, David was able to come back to India briefly. He took trips to Pakistan and Bangladesh, in order to spend time with Presbyterian mission personnel and strengthen relationships with our partner churches there. That also gave him the opportunity to attend Mary's high school graduation. I accompanied him to Pakistan, ten years after we had lived there, and was thrilled to see a fully operating private girls school,

Kinnaird Academy, which had only been in its dream stages when we left in 1997.

Our trip to Bangladesh was different. We went there for eight days to accompany Drs. Les and Cindy Morgan, after the tragic death of their twenty-five-year-old son to a rare form of bone cancer. They had taken a leave of absence and David had attended their son's funeral in Houston earlier that year. This visit was their trial run of returning to the mission field, after an experience of profound grief. Cindy had completed the Certificate of Spiritual Formation at Columbia Seminary and also a Spiritual Direction course through San Francisco Seminary. It was her desire to lead the four of us on a "spiritual retreat" while we were in Bangladesh, visiting the places of their ministry and service through the years they had served there. They had married and gone straight to Bangladesh. Cindy knew that when she married Les, she was also marrying Bangladesh!

What I did not anticipate was what happened to me while we traveled with these contemporary saints. I occasionally referred to them as "Mr. and Mrs. Jesus," a label they refused to embrace. Cindy structured our eight days to include a number of spiritual practices she had learned. She planned two days of intentional Sabbath rest, as well as inviting us to participate in the "Prayer of Examen" (St. Ignatius) each evening, when each of us would share our experiences of God's presence and absence during the day. On the Sabbath days, we participated in worship and Bible study in their home.

The first Bible study was a "Lectio-Divina" experience of the passage from Luke 8:40-56. Lectio-Divina is a guided meditation, where participants listen to a Bible story several times. The first time we simply listened. The second time, Cindy facilitated a guided meditation, which invited us to imagine where we were in the story. Were we people in the crowd? Were we disciples? Could we see and hear Jesus? She invited us to imagine and engage with Jesus as the group remained silent.

When we finished this experience and shared, I was overwhelmed with emotion. In the safety of the four persons gathered, I identified with the hemorrhaging woman. I was exhausted and losing blood metaphorically. Cindy responded pastorally and took me to another room to pray with me and talk through the experience. By my identifying with the woman who touched Jesus' garment and received healing, I recognized how truly exhausted and overwhelmed I was feeling. This homeless missionary/pastor, without a clear call, would be returning to India to sell off all of our possessions in an auction, would be saying goodbye to new friends and colleagues, and would be starting over one more time. The expectation of always pouring myself out and never being re-filled showed me that something needed to change. Our fast-paced life of mission and ministry never seemed to allow time for that deeper work.

I came to view our days in Bangladesh as a holy visit with God. I felt held and loved deeply by my Creator. God's healing touch and Cindy's spiritual practices led me to enroll in the Certificate of Spiritual Formation program at Pittsburgh Theological Seminary when we returned to the United States. I hungered and thirsted for a deeper experience of God's love, and looked

forward to diving into that program, as my way of spiritually tending my own heart and soul!

Questions for Reflection:

> ➤ *Can you describe a time when you could identify
>   closely with a Bible character or another person
>   of significance in your faith tradition?*

> ➤ *Describe a time in your life when you felt God was
>   absent. Describe a time in your life when you felt
>   God's presence in a tangible way.*

Chapter Fifteen:

Pushing the Re-Start Button

After returning to the United States in July 2009, I resided in Louisville, Kentucky, and continued in the Doctor of Ministry program. At the same time, I began the Spiritual Formation Certificate Program through Pittsburgh Theological Seminary, which involved short residencies at the seminary once or twice a year. I also dropped Mary off at Lake Forest College, north of Chicago, for her freshman year.

While in Louisville, I found myself unemployed with an empty nest, and a deep sense of anger and resentment about how my position was handled by the church, causing me to feel erased by the bureaucracy. I felt they were completely oblivious to the traumatic experience I had been through. Unlike our first year as missionaries, when there was a pastor for missionaries in the southern Presbyterian Church, after the reunion and formation of the Presbyterian Church (USA) in 1983, pastoral care of missionaries did not seem to be a priority. My meeting with the Executive Director and my "team" at the headquarters gave me closure, but many of my painful feelings remained unresolved.

In the months following my return, God was utterly faithful to provide for my needs. Brokenness and grace have been two sides of the same coin. Two courses I took that summer were, "Borders and Beyond" and

"Emotional Intelligence," which offered me needed opportunities to weep in a safe environment, where unconditional love was present. The professors and students in the classes were understanding of the trauma I had experienced and affirming of my gifts for ministry.

Adam Ruiz functioned in my life as an informal spiritual director. He first appeared to me (like an angel), one Friday afternoon on the seminary campus. I was feeling depressed and demoralized. He affirmed my unique gifts in cross-cultural ministry and invited me into relationships with Hispanic residents of Louisville. Adam was in the pastoral care track and is a seasoned, deeply spiritual listener, who heard me that day and accompanied me into places where my compassion and need could be connected to the needs, grief and dislocation of others. That same night he invited me to come as a guest to an open Hispanic Alcoholics Anonymous meeting at a nearby Catholic Church. On that particular day, when Adam invited me into this new world, I moved from deep depression to light-hearted laughter. It was a huge spiritual paradigm shift for me, from finding my worth in a "position" to finding my worth in my "personhood."

With Adam as my partner and friend, I navigated through the Doctor of Ministry Program and wrote my final paper on *Creating Safe Spaces for Grace "In Between" People with Cultural Differences,* a narrative of my experiences working with different Hispanic people living in Louisville. I interviewed all of them about their perceptions, including Adam. He gave me the feedback that I had veered towards the experience of the one most vulnerable individual; while, neglecting those who were professionals, to whom he had introduced me. That was important for me to hear, because to him, that felt like I was stereotyping the "down and out" Hispanics, rather than calling attention to those who were finding their niche in our culture. He would have done it differently, but as a respectful and wise counselor, he also knew that it was my narrative to tell and not his.

I also received excellent support from the readers of my dissertation, assigned to me by the seminary at the beginning of my research: Clifton Kirkpatrick, former Director of World Mission, and Claudio Carvalhaes, a professor of worship. Claudio, a native of Brazil, was the professor who created space for grace in my life when I was in between cultures, as a student in his class. By connecting my displacement with the displacement of Hispanic people in Louisville, God was building a bridge of grace in my life.

While in Louisville I enrolled in a Spiritual Immersion class, the first course to fulfill the Spiritual Formation Certificate program through Pittsburgh Seminary. For this class, I had to write a Spiritual Autobiography of my faith journey. We reflected on the seasons of our lives. It became clear to me during the course that my life had ebbed and flowed between two types of experiences, ones which stretched me out of my comfort zone in an extreme way, like a Class IV Rapids, and others that dropped me into a quiet, lonely pool, where I needed to collect myself and process the experiences. Living a fast-paced adventure of crossing cultures was exhilarating; however, those experiences alternated with times of loss and abandonment, where I found myself wet, cold, alone and exhausted. During this Immersion Class, I recognized my need to focus more intently on deepening my roots and grounding myself, becoming more centered in Christ, who wants to be the wellspring of my life that will never run dry.

As I looked back and reflected on these different chapters of my life, I felt both grateful and awed! God has tethered me to God's self and then flung me wide like one of those balls attached to the post in the middle. I've been tethered all along, spinning fast and wide and then closer to the post. What fun it has been and how terribly challenging as well! David has been my co-adventurer on this journey; however, he was not inclined to look back and catch me if I fell.

In fact, I remember when David was a seminary intern at Westminster Presbyterian Church in Charlotte, where he and I co-facilitated a youth camping trip. While creek hopping on the rocks with the youth, David was always at the front of the pack with the fastest youth, and I was always at the back, making sure no one got left behind. Sometimes I resented that. However, David has always been fully willing to leap with me and risk himself (and me!) for God's glory and for others in the broadest sense, which encompasses all of creation. Thank you, God, for this life partner! Our differentness has been both miserable and beautiful, both raw and holy.

One insight that arose in me while reading the *Invitation to a Journey: A Road Map for Spiritual Formation,* by M. Robert Mulholland Jr.,[12] was the importance of trusting our own inner voice, as God's spirit guiding us. What I discerned as I wrote my spiritual autobiography is that I have often deferred to David's strengths at the expense of my own. I have spent more time honoring

---

[12] M. Robert Mulholland, Jr., *Invitation to a Journey: A Road Map For Spiritual Formation.* (Downers Grove, Illinois: IVP Books), 1993.

and responding to his strengths, and not enough time honoring and developing my particular spiritual gifts. I need to give myself permission to take all the time I need to deepen my roots through spiritual practices, accentuating depth over breadth, for that is where I feel called. We have covered a lot of territory in our ministry. My hunger and thirst now are for deeper roots to sustain what has developed above ground.

My spiritual "mother" from Korea speaks to me from heaven, saying: "Stay on this course, Sue, and God will open doors for you. Cherish the reading, writing, praying and integrating of these life experiences. Lean into the community where you are present. Let others lean on you also. There's no hurry. Take all the time you need. There will be a place that allows you to be settled, to keep growing, and to serve. This new place will not burn you out, but will become a place, where you meet God, like the burning bush. "You will burn, but not be consumed. You will become holy ground, and people will encounter God in your company."

Questions for Reflection:

➢ *Do you tend to "trust" your inner voice, as the spirit of God speaking to you in a personal way?*

➢ *When you look back at the changing seasons of your life in the rear view mirror, do you experience regret, gratitude, or a mixture of both?*

Chapter Sixteen:

Finding My Footing

David encouraged me to seek a new call for myself, as I completed my Doctor of Ministry degree in Louisville. Although David's heart was rooted in God's work in Asia, doing that job while working out of the Louisville office was not ideal. When he accompanied me to St. Pauls, North Carolina, to be interviewed by the pastor nominating committee at St. Pauls Presbyterian Church, one member of the committee looked at David, and said, "This would be a lot easier, if we were calling you." I was not the first woman to serve at St. Pauls, but David quickly responded: "You are not talking to me; you are talking to my wife."

St. Pauls Presbyterian Church offered me the call and I accepted it. We moved into the house owned by the church, right next door to the church cemetery. The house was built by the first people to greet me on my first day of work. I recognized their names as being the son and daughter-in-law of the builder. Both T.J. Willis and his brother, Jerry, helped their father build the church and the manse. A former pastor, Rev. Dr. Joel Alvis, had written a 200th-anniversary short history of the church, which I read before preaching my first sermon at St. Pauls. That's how I knew who T.J. and Marie were when they walked in the door of the church.

Those were rich and meaningful years. Our family enjoyed many Christmases with plenty of space for children, grandparents and friends. The first Christmas we were there a lovely Muslim family from Yemen, who lived across the street, asked if they could join us for Christmas dinner. Knowing they do not eat ham, which was on our menu that evening, David ran out quickly to buy chicken. The family also showed up with pizza, so in a few short minutes, we shuffled all of the tables and utensils to make room for our interfaith neighbors! Our cross-cultural family made adjustments without a hitch. All the children gathered around the big kitchen table with the adults in the dining room. When I drove my father to the airport about a week later, he told me the high point of his Christmas that year was having Christmas dinner with our Muslim neighbors.

What led me to St. Pauls initially was the nearby location of an Hispanic worshipping community, called "Monte de los Olivos." Rev. Eduardo Moreno, an employee of our Presbytery, had helped to organize the group. Since my recent doctoral study had focused on cross-cultural partnership opportunities with the Hispanic people in Louisville, my heart was drawn to the possibility of doing bilingual events with our fellow Hispanic Presbyterians in St. Pauls. During the six years I served in that position, we held a number of bilingual worship services with the two congregations. I also had the privilege of baptizing some of their children, with our daughter, Rachel, a Spanish teacher, as my translator.

After the Hispanic worshipping community gave up their rental property, they held their services at our church for about six months, before the Presbytery assisted them in purchasing a property of their own in St. Pauls. For me, I would have loved the two congregations to become one family with two different services of worship, but both the English-speaking and the Spanish-speaking congregations did not share my vision. A high point of our partnership was when we invited them to St. Pauls' annual Homecoming Service on Mother's Day 2015. Our Hispanic sisters and brothers shared in our worship service and shared lunch on the lawn afterward.

If you do not mind fast-forwarding with me to March 1, 2020, I had the honor and privilege of preaching at the installation and ordination of Commissioned Ruling Elder, Pedro Garcia, a layperson who was trained by Rev. Eduardo Moreno, to serve as pastor of Monte de los Olivos. I was also asked to give the "Charge" to the congregation.

Having not seen many of those church members in four years, our reunion that evening was full of joy and celebration. The service lasted three hours! Everyone was invited to stay for dinner in the Fellowship Hall!

Questions for Reflection:

> ➤ *When have you had a dream or a vision that was a little "ahead of its time"?*

> ➤ *Describe a time in your life when you had the privilege of seeing the "fruit" of your labor many years after the fact.*

St. Pauls Presbyterian Church Homecoming 2015

A Legacy of Healing Love

*B*ecause of David's previous connections as the Asia Coordinator for the Presbyterian Church (USA), we were invited to be guests of Yodogawa Christian Hospital in Japan to celebrate the opening of a new facility in Osaka, with all expenses paid by the hospital. The architectural design of the new facility included a large, ornate chapel at the center of the complex, symbolizing the hospital's commitment to its Christian roots and whole-person healing.[13]

It was a delightful trip, which highlighted a long partnership between the Presbyterian Church (USA) and Christians in Japan. In 2009 Pat Cole wrote an article about this partnership because Yodogawa Christian Hospital gave back to the Presbyterian Church (USA) $208,577 to be used for mission work in Asia. This gift represented the same amount of money that Presbyterian Women contributed in 1956 to Yodogawa, which was founded by Presbyterian Church (USA) missionaries. This Presbyterian Women's Birthday Offering in 1956 helped build a 76-bed hospital that has now grown into a multi-faceted medical complex.

According to Cole, "The Presbyterian medical ministry in Osaka began in 1955 when missionaries

---

[13] Pat Cole, Presbyterian Church (USA) Mission Agency, October 1, 2009.

opened the Yodogawa Christian Clinic. The first super-intendent, Dr. Frank Brown, committed Yodogawa to provide 'whole person healing' in an impoverishcd community still reeling from World War II. Brown retired in the late 1970s, but Yodogawa's dedication to a visible Christian witness has continued under Japanese leadership, even though only about two percent of the Japanese population is Christian."[14]

David reported to the General Assembly Mission Council on September 24, 2009 and is quoted in Cole's article as saying: "It's a story that began in Osaka, Japan, after the Second World War, and it's a story that continues in Osaka, where Yodogawa is one of the primary medical facilities in a city that is second in population (in Japan) only to Tokyo." David highlighted that the hospital is one of the top private hospitals in Japan, with eight facilities: three hospitals, two clinics, two geriatric care facilities and a health promotion center. Yodogawa now has 657 beds and a staff of 1,000.

Dr. Masaaki Mukubo, Yodogawa's superintendent, said that "Yodogawa Christian Hospital was once a recipient of God's love from the PC(USA), and it is our mission now to pass it on to other Asian countries that are in need." This was one of several large mission gifts to the PC(USA). Yodogawa has also provided direct aid to hospitals in Bangladesh, Nepal and China.

Being invited as guests to the opening of the new facility in 2012 was an extraordinary opportunity for us to see the fruit of God's love coming to maturity in a country where Christians are in the minority according

[14] Ibid.

to population, but who offer to the whole country the gifts of wholistic healing in the name of Jesus Christ.

Questions for Reflection:

1) *Where have you seen the fruit of God's love, which was the result of many years or generations of discipleship?*

2) *How do you understand the concept of "wholistic healing," and when have you experienced healing which impacted you physically, mentally, emotionally and/or spiritually?*

Parenting Pop-Pop

While still on route back to St. Pauls from Japan, I had a series of missed calls from my Uncle Hank in Pittsburgh, who never calls me. I had my phone turned off while overseas and picked up the voicemails in the first airport where we landed in the United States. I called him back to learn that he had some serious concerns about my father's health and well-being. My dad was eighty-nine years old and was still living alone at home in the house where I grew up. He was a stubborn and independent man, even cantankerous, but according to my Uncle Hank, he had arrived at Hank's house on a Thursday night to pick Hank up for a breakfast meeting with a financial consultant. Dad was confused about the time, the day and where he was going.

From that day forward, David and I went into full alert that something had to be done and most likely we would be called upon to take responsibility. Dad visited us over Thanksgiving and Christmas, as he normally did. We urged my brother, in Pittsburgh, to get involved and take Dad to some medical doctors for their assessments when he was back in Pittsburgh, which he did.

In January of 2013, my dad's older sister, Jane, passed away, so I flew to Pittsburgh for the funeral, which gave me an opportunity to check on dad. My brother drove me back to the airport for the return trip to North Carolina, but we were not sure how dad's story would unfold. Only one month later, I received a call from a policeman in the middle of a Saturday night in February. He found my number on the blotter of my dad's desk. Apparently, Dad had left the house with the front door wide open, not wearing the appropriate clothing for a twenty-degree night in Pittsburgh. He was looking for his car by walking in the direction of his church. The road curved and on the left side of the road was a fenced-in cemetery. A woman stopped to assist my dad, offering him a blanket. She called the police, who came and took Dad to St. Clair Hospital for observation. The policeman had returned to Dad's house to secure it and call next of kin. My brother did not answer the phone, so I was the next in line. I thanked the man profusely for taking care of my dad and closing up the house. I told him I would contact the hospital and do what needed to be done.

What a wake-up call that was! As it turned out, I spoke a number of times to my brother, who visited Dad in the hospital. We hoped that Dad could be released to an assisted living facility; however, because he had not been officially admitted to the hospital, but was only being held for observation, we could not require that he be released to a care facility. My brother and his wife, Patsy, took Dad home, took his car keys, and offered to do any errands for him the next day. Patsy spent the first night with Dad to make sure he was okay and then headed home the next day.

When she came back a day or so later to take him grocery shopping, his car was gone. We found out later that Dad had a spare key and found it. He would not be one to give up his freedom without a fight! I was thinking about flying to Pittsburgh to take charge of my dad's care; however, David encouraged me to wait and let my brother be the responsible party for the time being, since Lent was beginning and my responsibilities as the pastor of St. Pauls were heavy.

David and I made the decision to go to Pittsburgh the Monday after Easter to pick up my dad and bring him to North Carolina. When we took him out to dinner the night we arrived, he had to go to the men's room at the restaurant and was coughing up mucus. We made the decision to take him to North Carolina permanently, even though he did not know that was what we were doing! He expected that we were taking him to North Carolina for a short vacation. During that week we met with Dad's lawyer and financial advisor and discovered that he had not dealt with his taxes for 2012. Dad told me he no longer had to file taxes. We gathered all the paperwork, which was sitting right beside his desk, and took him to North Carolina that same week in 2013. My dad, a life-long resident of Mount Lebanon, never returned to Pittsburgh and never had the opportunity to say goodbye to anyone.

Having Dad in our home changed our lives dramatically. One week after we picked up Dad, a sixty-year-old elder in my church died unexpectedly. While managing Dad, I supported the elder's wife and family and prepared the funeral service that week. When I sat down and exhaled after the funeral was over, we learned that David's mother was in the hospital. Rebekah was the last person to visit her that evening. David had seen her earlier in the week but planned to go visit the next day also. She died during the night unexpectedly. We all traveled to Charlotte for Cora Ann's funeral that Saturday. David and his brothers coordinated the details of the funeral service with the senior pastor at Covenant Presbyterian, the church where both his mother and father had been charter members. David's mom was a long-time member of the choir, so a number of choir members came to sing for her service. I did not stand in line with the family, greeting people who attended her funeral, because I stayed with my father to watch out for him, and make sure he did not wander away.

When we returned from Charlotte to St. Pauls the night of Cora Ann's funeral, I literally started walking out of town towards the beach to escape my own life. I had left my phone and money behind and walked six miles before I decided that it was not a good idea. I stopped at a big church and bumped into the custodian on a Saturday evening when the sun was setting. She let me call David on her phone, provided some precious, feminine pastoral care, and let me sit in her car until David arrived to pick me up. I picked up a brochure on a table in the narthex of her church on "How to Care for a Parent with Dementia." David had to drive around for quite a while, before I agreed to go home. How unfair it was that I was breaking down on the night of my husband's mother's funeral. I was ashamed and broken and wanted to die. But sure enough, we both had to wake up the next morning and go preach sermons at our respective churches, which we did.

As the days passed, we took Dad for an evaluation with a neuropsychologist in Pinehurst, who specializes in geriatric patients. Dad was diagnosed with mixed dementia: Alzheimer's and Lewy Body. While we were juggling ministry in three churches between the two of us, we were also caring for my dad. He could be a feisty fellow. One day he decided to take a walk over to the police station in St. Pauls to report that we had kidnapped him. Fortunately, David followed him there and shared the letter from Dad's doctor about his diagnosis. Ray was healthy as a horse physically, so he resisted his loss of mental acumen at every turn. We put him temporarily in an Assisted Living Facility to attend Mary's college graduation. However, two days after we left, Dad was picked up trying to hitchhike back to Pittsburgh. A staff member at the assisted living facility picked him up and put him into the locked unit for people with dementia.

During the first year of Dad's living in North Carolina, I recognized that I was in over my head emotionally and needed to get help for myself. I participated in a program at First Health in Pinehurst, North Carolina, called, "Mindfulness-Based Stress Reduction Meditation (MBSR)," which utilizes Jon Kabat Zinn's book, *Full Catastrophe Living.*[15] It is a practical program initiated at the University of Massachusetts Medical School, where Zinn was a professor of medicine. I made the trip from St. Pauls to Pinehurst every Monday night for eight weeks to practice two hours of meditation as a way of grounding myself for the long journey ahead. We found dad an excellent geriatric specialist. At one appointment, I asked (pleaded), "How long, doctor?"

He smiled and responded, "Well, Sue, I am not God..."

---

[15] Jon Kabat Zinn, *Full Catastrophe Living: Using the Wisdom of Your Body and Mind to Face Stress, Pain, and Illness.* (New York: New York, Bantam Dell, A Division of Random House, Inc.), 1990.

I replied, "Nor am I. But you have much more experience with the process of this disease. Can you take a guess?"

He answered, "I don't think it will be more than five years."

During our years in St. Pauls, Dad stayed in an assisted living facility for about six months in the locked-down unit as a result of his hitchhiking expedition. In the hopes that we might get a second chance at putting him in an Assisted Living Facility that would not require him to be in the locked unit with patients much more physically challenged than he was, we brought him home with us for another try. He stayed with us for several months.

One night in December I was in charge of taking the youth Christmas caroling to the homes of older members of the church. Our next door neighbors were going to bring my dad to the party at the end of the evening at another church member's home. After singing to the mother of one of our church members in a house across the street from the church, I saw my dad wandering around outside the church's main entrance. We drove over and I invited him into the van with us. When we stopped at the home of a blind man in his nineties, we left Dad there to talk and socialize while we finished caroling. I went back to get Dad before the party. When we arrived at the party, everyone was in a panic because my next door neighbors could not find my dad and the door to our home, the church manse, was wide open. When I arrived with Dad, everyone was relieved, delighted and exuberant that he was okay.

As the months passed, we realized that, for his safety and our sanity, we needed to put him in another

Assisted Living Facility, one where he had his own room and could come and go a little more freely, but also receive meals and supervision. He was fine there until the day after Thanksgiving. David's father and my father spent Thanksgiving with us in our home in St. Pauls. David took my dad home the next day. Before the day ended, my dad had taken flight again. He got lost and walked into a nearby hotel on a busy road. Dad showed the staff at the hotel his wrist band from the Assisted Living facility, which helped them get him back to the Assisted Living facility, but that was the end of his freedom. He was moved into their locked unit, where he lived during the remaining time that I served as a pastor in St. Pauls.

Questions for Reflection:

> *Have you had the experience of parenting one of your own parents?*

> *What did you learn about yourself, while you shouldered that responsibility?*

Chapter Nineteen

Spiritual Pilgrimage to Bangladesh

During our years in St. Pauls, I tried to take at least one course for the Certificate in Spiritual Formation as part of my Continuing Education every year; however, I transferred my program from Pittsburgh to Columbia Seminary in Decatur, Georgia, since it was closer to where we lived. One requirement in the program involved planning a "Practicum," which could have been a class for elders, a woman's retreat, or some other church program, implementing what I had learned in the program. During one of my classes in Montreat, I met a woman who did her "Practicum" in Taiwan, where she had served as a missionary. That knowledge planted a seed in my heart that perhaps I could integrate my mission and ministry roles, by offering a Spiritual Pilgrimage to Bangladesh, where our friends, Doctors Les and Cindy Morgan, were still serving. Each "Practicum" requires a Supervisor, who is someone familiar with the Spiritual Formation Certificate Program, which Cindy had already completed.

The leaders at Columbia were open to this idea, and Cindy welcomed the opportunity to assist me in planning an itinerary in Bangladesh, while also serving as my Supervisor. A friend and former church member from Bethesda, and a couple, who were friends and church members in St. Pauls, signed on for the adventure! With Les and Cindy as part of the group, we were a group of six pilgrims for a total of nineteen days in September 2015.

The idea of coordinating a pilgrimage to Bangladesh with church members and friends from the United States was one way I hoped to integrate my own overseas experiences as a missionary with my experiences of ministry within my own country. God had led David and me out of the United States on numerous occasions, as we listened to the Spirit's movement in our lives. I had a deep desire to share that cross-cultural experience with people I knew and loved within my own culture. Some friends and family members have viewed David and me as gypsies, or pilgrims, from the get-go of our marriage and careers. The practice of "letting go" and "letting God" has been part of our family's DNA from the day we said, "I do."

Cindy accepted my invitation with joy and also took responsibility for planning our itinerary in Bangladesh, since it was her country and her calling that would serve as the backdrop, location, host culture, language and characters for this spiritual journey. Who willingly embraces such a task? Drs. Les and Cynthia Morgan sincerely and humbly seek to embody the mystery of Christ's love, wherever they are called to serve.

I began journaling in July when our family took a vacation at the beach, as a way of preparing myself spiritually. Cindy recommended that I read Phil

Cousineau's *The Art of Pilgrimage.*[16] In his forward, Huston Smith writes: "We need to be centered in ourselves, not somewhere in the outer world. The person who is always expecting consolation from without is like a swaying reed or a boat on a stormy sea."[17]

When I last spoke to my Spiritual Director before the trip, she noted that it sounded like I was giving her a travelogue, like a Christian educator, which I am! She challenged me, saying: "Pilgrimage is different than a Christian educational program. Sue, you need to go much deeper within yourself, where you will be grounded and ready for God's unfolding." This is the centeredness I was seeking, which Cindy called: "deep calling to deep." Cousineau recommends that the "secret of soulful travel is to believe there is something sacred waiting to be discovered. The 'art' of pilgrimage is the art of seeing the sacred – being fully awake and aware. Soaking everything in, seeing, hearing, touching, walking, being—with humility."[18]

Before our group left, these were my prayers for each pilgrim. "Lord, I pray you will surround Laura Murdock and help her name the question that she is leaning into and seeking. Is there a 'normal' for which her heart longs? Can she find you in the center of her being?"

"Lord, I lift up Vivian, as she grieves the recent loss of her mother. She feels raw and does not want to fall apart while she travels. I cannot name her need, her

---

[16] Phil Cousineau, *The Art of Pilgrimage: The Seeker's Guide to Making Travel Sacred.* (San Francisco, CA: Conari Press, an imprint of Red Wheel/Weiser, LLC), 1998, p. xii.

[17] Ibid., p. xii.

[18] Ibid.

question, or her longing, but I pray that you will meet her where she is, Lord, and free her, loosening her up to experience all sides of life."

"Lord, I lift up Bill, whose heart also hungers, who is not sure what 'transformation' would look like; yet, he is thrilled, eager and embracing the journey at perhaps the deepest level of all."

"Lord, I lift up Les. May his 'man heart' be touched and illuminated. He is a deeply Spirt-filled man, whom I respect. May his prayer partnership with Bill Millar be transformative/illuminating/joyful! May they connect in a mutually inspiring way."

"And of course, Lord, I pray for Cindy, my beloved and beautiful sister in Christ, who is 'illuminative' in her being. Allow her to experience our spiritual practices and find her deepest longings awakened, aware, confirmed. Speak deep truth in her and through her on this trip. Thank you for her commitment to me and this project, Lord. I am awed by it and by her and by You in her."

One week before the Spiritual Pilgrimage, I set up a full-size labyrinth, which would be a metaphor for our entire journey together. I invited our state-side pilgrims: Vivian, Bill and Laura to walk the labyrinth before our departure, as preparation for the pilgrimage. A labyrinth is one path, not a maze, but a mindful, slow walk on the same path in silence. The purpose of walking the path is to redirect our focus, time, attention and priorities away from what normally consumes us.

The canvas labyrinth filled up the entire Fellowship Hall floor at St. Pauls Presbyterian Church. I had worked all day to set up the physical space and still did not feel ready when 4:00 p.m. arrived. The physical preparation allowed minimal time for spiritual discernment of how the two-hour session would unfold, so I had to go with the flow in the moments of leading the group.

During this first meeting, there were some important moments of awareness. For Laura, the monsoon of rain that poured down, leading up to the time of the meeting, was a kind of "baptism," commissioning her for this trip overseas. Laura's tears and fears as she walked out of the center of the labyrinth reflected her fears of returning home to the life she was leaving behind to travel with us.

Bill's reluctance to begin the journey and then his swift exit from the center of the labyrinth, where he felt claustrophobic, seemed to reflect his need for privacy and finding God in the silence. His need for space was critical to his re-creation in God's love. Vivian had a meditative, joyful, soulful walk as she recited the Jesus' prayer, singing: "Spirit of the Living God." She was also noticing what others were doing and where they were.

I was experimenting with an imaginary cup or bowl, and my desire for the Lord to keep refilling it. I also felt crowded in the center and had a desire to laugh out loud. I was mindful of the quiet, creaking floor and the huge spaciousness of the room, as well as the fewness of our group. I also felt the weight of responsibility I was undertaking. I felt some trepidation about dragging people into this experience, with very little orientation to a third-world, developing country. Laura, Bill and Vivian all assured me at dinner that they were adults and were choosing the pilgrimage. God is the Supervisor, not Sue. God was inviting us onto sacred ground and into "Xairos" time, which is a Greek word for "time" that focuses more on the significance of the moment, rather than chronological time. We all accepted God's invitation.

As the meeting began, I lit a candle and gave out a paper that explained the journey of a labyrinth. Then we experienced ten minutes of sitting meditation, led by Jon Kabat Zinn, using a Mindfulness Based Stress Reduction CD. I also read the Scripture from John 4:4-42, about Jesus meeting the Samaritan woman at the well, which would be the central scripture for our pilgrimage. After that, we did our labyrinth walk and also debriefed the experience.

Cindy sent us a video from Bangladesh about the devastating fires and collapse at the Rana Plaza, a clothing factory, which produced clothing for Walmart, Gap and other well-known stores in the United States. We also de-briefed the video, which was deeply disturbing. All the people who lost their lives were never compensated for losses, even though the clothing they were producing was made for overseas companies.

Finally, we read Colossians 3 about "wearing/putting on Christ," and talked about the importance of "taking off the old self" in order to put on compassion for the journey ahead. The metaphor of changing clothes physically, which the women in our group would have to do to be culturally appropriate in Bangladesh and India, also implied that we needed to make some changes in ourselves spiritually, as we entered into a completely different culture.

After the two-hour meeting, we ate supper together in St. Pauls. I was famished, overwhelmed and depleted, but the experiences of my fellow pilgrims made it all worth it. I felt weak, emptied, and somewhat insecure about what I was preparing to do. It was a "weak week"! However, in that weakness, God strengthened me, by providing some "holy" conversations with the ladies at the Presbytery office, where I secured the canvas labyrinth, and with my friend, Kathleen, who had already completed the Spiritual Formation Certificate Program.

During that same week, my dad had a fall and spent the day in the hospital with Vivian attending him. The Emergency Room doctor telephoned me directly to talk about what it's like to have a parent with Alzheimer's, which was another God moment for me. The doctor reassured me that my pilgrimage needed to go forward. I was able to accept the distraction of the pilgrimage as a gift and an opportunity to let go of control, as I allowed Vivian to minister to both me and my dad on that day. She is good in the Emergency Room and in companioning those who are suffering. I was emotional but let my small village minister to me that week.

When we finally arrived in Dhaka, Bangladesh on September 7, 2015, we spent our first night at the Super Hotel. We had to switch rooms when my bed turned out to be infested with cockroaches, but Dr. Leslie Morgan came to the rescue and communicated with the hotel staff that a change was needed. The next morning we did our first gathering at Cindy's and Les' home. We read the passage from Philippians 2 about Jesus Christ emptying himself to be God's representative in human flesh. We reflected upon our weaknesses as opportunities for God to be our strength. Later that afternoon, we each answered the question: "What is my desire for this pilgrimage?"

Laura shared that she did want something different in her life. She was stepping out of her comfort zone to encounter God and was seeking deeper commitment in her relationships. Bill did not have an answer to the question. He just wanted the next step but said he was fully present. Vivian said it was a time of transition in her life. She was emotionally raw, experiencing both retirement and the loss of her mother, which left her feeling depleted. She was seeking the return of joy into her life. Cindy was bringing a "Beginner's Mind," since they had been in Bangladesh for twenty-seven years. She wanted to see Bangladesh with fresh eyes on this journey. Les was seeking sustainability for himself and for their work, which had been hard and they were tired. We closed with prayer.

Without going into all of the details of our pilgrimage, there were many highs and lows for each person on the trip. What was particularly interesting for me, as the facilitator of the group, was the fact that no one person experienced the same thing, even though we all traveled together and stayed together for the entire journey. What was a high point or God moment for one pilgrim, was someone else's least favorite experience. Like the labyrinth, no two of our journeys, even though we were all on the same path, were the same.

After saying goodbye to Les and Cindy in Dhaka, we had one more segment of our pilgrimage. We spent four days in India, where Delhi was once home to me. As I stood in the Indira Gandhi International Airport with three fellow travelers from the United States, waves of poignant nostalgia arose in me, like tides on the outer banks of North Carolina. It was a joy to be greeted by my dear friends, Shanti and Berti Devadas, and to move back into the familiar rooms of the YMCA.

Our first outing was to Shimla from Delhi on an overnight train to get a glimpse of the Himalaya Mountains.
After two nights in Shimla, we returned to Delhi where
we were hosted by the Devadas family. We searched
out the apartment where I had once lived, saw the historic sites where Mahatma Gandhi was memorialized
and did some shopping. We also ate delicious Indian
food. On the Sunday before we departed, we attended
the Free Church, Parliament Street with the Devadas
family. Getting around Delhi seemed luxurious and
cosmopolitan after our time in Bangladesh.

As we reentered Indira Gandhi airport for the last
time, I had time to do some deeper reflection about
what each of us had experienced on our intense and
concentrated spiritual pilgrimage. There were moments
along the way when each one of us experienced darkness, which St. Ignatius describes as a feeling of "God's
absence," rather than presence. How did each of us work
through those moments? Wasn't a spiritual journey
designed to grow faith, not extinguish it, deepen roots,
not destroy them? As we boarded the plane one of us
had a seat separated from the other three. I asked for
that separate seat to give myself space to reflect and
process how the trip had impacted me personally.

Once seated, I journaled fast and furiously about
all we had seen and witnessed. There were many deep
and profound moments, like Bill's moving encounter
with God at the Sisters of Charity orphanage in Dhaka.
We were invited to walk around and hold some of the
babies. We chose to do this in silence without having
conversations with each other, as a form of prayerful
meditation for the babies. That evening Bill emotionally

described that while he was holding "his baby," he sensed that his baby was praying for him.

The time we spent in Bangladesh was intense beyond words. It was not my country or language; however, Cindy and Les had invited us into their world and had given us a taste of the challenges facing the Church of Bangladesh in a majority Muslim country. They had led us through Dhaka's darkest ghettos, where we stopped and said prayers for babies, elderly women and men, orphans, and the disabled. We had met with students studying in a small Christian seminary, who had come from remote villages and ethnic minorities.

We had lunch with the Bishop and other church leaders who shared with us the challenges they faced. We saw the "empty hole" where a garment factory had once stood, but because of poor construction and lack of safety precautions, it had collapsed with all of its workers inside. We lit candles on the site and met relatives of some of the deceased who had never been compensated for their losses.

We traveled by trains, buses and rickshaws into the rural areas, where we saw hostels and schools run by the Church of Bangladesh. The students did dances, and we passed out small color-coded bells to children, guiding them to ring Christian hymns they recognized, without their having to read music. We worshipped in a Taizé community that supported women's cooperatives, such as a carpet making shop for disabled women and a group home for adults with mental disabilities. There were too many God moments to count.

Our most enchanting adventure was the two-hour bicycle rickshaw ride to a remote village near the border of Bangladesh and India, where only the Bishop's quarters had a generator for electricity. We gave that room to Bill and Vivian. For Laura and me, our time in the remote village of Panihatta, where the entire village came out to greet us on the road when we arrived, was a divine encounter. On Saturday night, I led very brief devotions as we walked the Fourteen Stations of the Cross. I spoke in English; Cindy translated into Bangla, and local villagers translated into local dialects. We all carried candles in the darkness, as we made our way up the mountain together.

The next morning, I had the privilege of serving communion side by side with the local priest, who fed us in his home the day before. We gave him and his community a communion chalice and paten, which I had received at the time of my ordination. It was our gift to these sisters and brothers in Christ. I led them in a communal "Chalice Prayer" as the service con-cluded, where we joined hands with one another, lifted them up to God and asked God to fill us as a commu-nity with overflowing love for the world. Cindy and Les' many years of building relationships in Bangladesh with indigenous Christian people were condensed into two weeks for us to experience. It was their offering and their lives broken open for us.

Dr. M. Craig Barnes, presently serving as President of Princeton Theological Seminary, explains in his book, *Sacred Thirst: Meeting God in the Desert of our Longings,* that God searches for us, but we sometimes miss those moments of encounter, because our expectations are dashed rather than fulfilled. When each of my fellow pilgrims experienced moments of fear, loss, or dark-ness on the trip, I felt responsible for their suffering or struggles. Cindy pointed this out to me along the way, that I needed to trust that God was working, even when it was not visible to me. Growing in faith always includes times of consolation and times of desolation. As the "spiritual shepherd" for our group, it was hard for me to allow my "sheep" to go through moments of desolation along the way. However, Barnes goes on to say: "The hope supplied in and through Jesus Christ is not easy to contain and it is certainly not what we expected. [God] frequently surprises us and, yes, sometimes disappoints us." God tirelessly seeks us, Barnes continues, "but the gate to God's Kingdom is so narrow that you can't fit through unless you drop all your expectations – and maybe the briefcase that has too much work in it."[19]

I was grateful to be home. I was greeted by my partner in mission and ministry, David, who fully understood my exhaustion in introducing cross-cultural ministry to people who had never before been expected to take off their cultural clothes in order to "put on Christ" in a foreign land. As my fellow pilgrims debriefed a few weeks later and walked the outdoor labyrinth by Hospice House in Pinehurst, we were able to discuss our experiences of desolation more objectively, as well as the highpoints of the journey. We realized that God had been with us through both the highs and the lows.

Although I expected that our group would make a presentation of our pilgrimage to our home churches, as David and I did so many times when we returned from missionary service, these pilgrims were not ready to share their experiences in a public setting. Five years

---

[19] Dr. M. Craig Barnes, *Sacred Thirst: Meeting God in the Desert of Our Longings*, (Grand Rapids, Michigan: Zondervan), 2001, p. 108.

later, whenever I talk to Vivian, Bill and Laura about Bangladesh, they acknowledge it was life-changing. Laura was touched deeply by the hospitality of people who have so little. Each one of us was broken and put back together numerous times during the experience, including me. I have remained friends with Doctors Les and Cindy Morgan, who have retired from Bangladesh, and are now writing the next chapter of their lives, as they reintegrate into American culture, and have more time to spend with their family.

Questions for Reflection:

➢ *When have you bitten off something that was almost too big to chew, as I did, when I dreamed about and implemented a Spiritual Pilgrimage to Bangladesh?*

➢ *What experience in your life has had the greatest impact on your spiritual life, and did that experience include any times of desolation, as ours did?*

Chapter Twenty

Saying Goodbye and Hello One More Time

David and I pastored three churches during those years, while we lived in St. Pauls. They were enriching years, where I had the privilege of serving as a solo pastor, which I deeply appreciated. Our daughters visited home often and felt warmly welcomed and loved by the St. Pauls Presbyterian congregation. Rachel's fluency in Spanish gave me many opportunities to try out bilingual worship services and to participate in Spanish services, where she served as my translator. She told me that I am not easy to translate for, because I like to speak in metaphors and use fresh words that cannot always be translated directly into another language.

However, with my dad living full time in Moore County in an Alzheimer's unit, about an hour's drive from St. Pauls, God began to nudge me to move closer to where he was. David and I were also pulled in many different directions during those years. Since we served in three churches, that meant three weeks of Vacation Bible School every summer, three Session meetings every month, three Homecomings, and pastoral visitation. We attended three Valentine dinners every year in February and if you multiply every church program times three, you might imagine that sharing one congregation would look attractive. I also missed David's complementary ministry gifts and looked forward to renewing that partnership.

We learned that Bethesda Presbyterian Church was also seeking new pastoral leadership. Since two of our children had graduated from high school in Southern Pines, the thought of going home to Bethesda sounded like a refreshing change. In our absence, Bethesda went through some difficult times. The timing of their need, our desire and God's guidance reunited us to that congregation one more time!

The most poignant moment for me was a Sunday afternoon in March 2016, when Bethesda had a Called Congregational Meeting to present their desire to offer a call to David and me to return to serve as their pastors. In the Presbyterian system, this process is kept very quiet and under the radar. So on the very same day that Bethesda was celebrating our return, I had to break the news to the Session at St. Pauls that I would be leaving. My soul could barely contain the mixture of grief and joy, which I experienced on that day. I actually received the phone call from a member of the Search Committee at Bethesda, while I was sitting in the ladies' parlor at St. Pauls waiting for the Session members to show up and be informed of my departure. I walked outside to receive the news, which caused my heart to leap for joy, and then had to walk back into the parlor at St. Pauls to deliver the sad news. My heart ached at that moment. It was almost more than I could bear. I loved the people of St. Pauls Presbyterian Church with all of my heart; however, I also knew that God was leading us in a new direction.

David and I were invited back to serve as pastors at Bethesda after nine years had passed. The transition from St. Pauls, North Carolina, back to Aberdeen, North Carolina, was grueling. David and his hardworking buddies labored into the wee hours of the morning preparing the "Cooper House" for us, which was a rental house owned by the church. Jim Ransdell brought a trailer to make the final move from St. Pauls. Bill Rock was still securing towel racks in the renovated bathroom when we arrived about midnight to unload. We finally laid our heads down at about 2:00 a.m. Friday morning on Poplar Street, two doors down from the church. We arrived: alive, exhausted, and blessed beyond belief.

A few hours later, on Friday morning, the husband of a life-long church member passed away. Ministry does not take a rest. Welcome home. Fortunately, a few church members had whispered in our ears the names of people who needed immediate pastoral care, so that we were able to visit folks who passed away during our first weeks on the job. We hit the job running on very little sleep.

Questions for Reflection:

> ➤ *How do you know when God is calling you in a new direction? Is it difficult to trust that call?*

> ➤ *Describe a time in your life when saying goodbye and hello was a mixture of grief and joy.*

Chapter Twenty-One:

Settled Yet?

After nine months of living in the church rental house on Poplar Street, we began to search for a place to settle down and call our own. Rebekah had her "new properties-for-sale-app" activated on her phone and would contact us with places to visit. Just days before Christmas, she alerted us to a home for sale with a swimming pool in the backyard. My heart leapt for joy at the prospect of living there. We were the first to look at the house. The day after Christmas, we took David's father to see it, and he gave it a thumbs up! As the first people to make an offer, we could not offer too low a price, or they would pass over us and wait for someone else. David suggested it may be too much house for us at our age. Even my Spiritual Director suggested: "Wouldn't you, at your age, prefer to be down-sizing rather than up-sizing?"

Were those two collaborating? My response was visceral. To David, I said, "You have not had a single health problem and you also love working in the yard. How could it be too much? You are not condo-material yet." To my Spiritual Director, I responded by saying: "With all due respect to your wisdom, you don't know how we have spent most of our thirty-seven years of marriage. We have lived in single rooms and missionary apartments both overseas and in the United States. We have shared space in other peoples' homes, including our parents' homes. We have only lived in a home of our own eight of those thirty-seven years."

"This is what I need! This is what God wants for us!" My very soul was shouting, but trusting my inner voice, when the voices of people I respect are saying something different, is difficult for me. My Spiritual Director advised me to trust my voice. She apologized for imagining what she would prefer, rather than hearing my needs, which may be different than everyone else's around me. I took her at her word and have been trying hard, failing, and trying again to listen to my inner voice and God's voice within me. What a roller coaster experience it has been since that decision was made!

We purchased the home and made the transition the weekend of Palm Sunday. On Monday morning, April 10, 2017, I wrote in my journal: "I sit in the backyard of our new home with deep gratitude to You, O Lord! I see this home as a well of rest, refreshment and renewal. I delight in the birds singing, the pink azaleas blooming, the dogwood blossoms greening for the summer. It is a glorious day, O Lord."

I received a message the day before that my dad had taken a turn for the worse during the week of our move when I had not had the chance to visit as regularly as I normally did. The staff at the nursing home thought I needed to know. Sunday evening, April 9th, and Monday evening, April 10th were my last two visits with Dad. I called my kids on Sunday to alert them to the fact that I believed Dad was passing away during Holy Week. On Monday, when Dad could not swallow the oatmeal cookie I brought him from Panera, I knew his time was growing shorter. I hugged him, kissed him and prayed with him. He passed away at 2:20 in the afternoon on Tuesday the following day, while I was providing pastoral care for a family whose son was having brain surgery in Chapel Hill. David sat with Dad's body until I arrived.

We created a Service of Celebration for Good Friday, April 14, 2017, at Bethesda, and then traveled as a family to Pittsburgh, where we celebrated Ray Bower's life again in his home church, Mt. Lebanon United Presbyterian Church. He was laid to rest before the service beside my mother in Mt. Lebanon Cemetery. The love and affirmations of our family and dad's friends, especially his hometown running buddies, along with Charles Allie (a world-class runner), and his football officiating buddies, were so gratifying and gave me closure. Yes, dad had finished his race and received his prize!

After returning home from Pittsburgh and resuming work at Bethesda – many people asked me: "Are you settled yet?" On May 24, 2017, I penned this poem:

Settled yet?

People ask me this question.
It makes me want to
run away.

I love my home.
I want to retreat here.
I long for "settled-ness."
God, please settle my heart
this morning.
God, please find me, as you found
the blindman in our Bible story this week.

"Do you know what I have done for you?"
Jesus asked his disciples
… after washing their feet.
The next day he died.

In your physical absence,
Lord, the Holy Spirit
came and took up
residence in them,
settled IN them.
Will you settle in me, Lord?
Will you be my life partner?
I want to be yours.

"Sue, I have called you 'Friend,'
Remain in me and
I will be in you.

I was grateful beyond words that we had moved into our house before Dad passed away. Although he never saw our home, he would have loved to put his feet in our swimming pool. But settling down for me remained unsettling. We hired a pool professional, named Josh, to open and prepare our pool for the summer season, but this was new ground for all of us. I watched carefully as Josh and his co-workers cleaned and freshened the pool. It was a long process.

When Settling Down is Unsettling

My first year as owner
of a pool...
I want it to become
my dolphin cove
of tranquility.

I watch Josh
nurture her inert waters
back to health and clarity.
The algae of anger,
uncovered for the first time,
is thick, green, cloudy.

No one knows how long it will
take to shock and vacuum
away the year's debris.

I, like her,
have been uncovered this spring.
My heart needs clearing and
aches for purity from hidden angers,
delayed grief, perceived slights and
over-functioning.

"My soul is at rest
in God alone.
My salvation
comes from God."[20]

Clearly, it was going to take some time for me to settle down, not just physically, but mentally, emotionally and spiritually. Dad's passing away was the end of a long chapter of caregiving. Dad's doctor had estimated not longer than five years. It turned out to be four years for David and me to be his caregivers. It was a privilege and it was also draining. It was going to take me some time to find a new normal and to feel rejuvenated.

Questions for Reflection:

➢ *Is there anything "unsettled" in your life or your heart right now?*

➢ *When and how has God uncovered things in your life and heart that needed attention?*

---

[20] Taizé song, "My Soul is at Rest."

RAFT #3:

The Raft of Inner Healing

Chapter One

Unplugged with Purpose

The next raft I am inviting you to board with me will revisit some of the chronological places where we have already traveled. This is the raft of inner healing, where I will share some of the inside stories of my heart, that have been bubbling beneath the surface of the outer journey for several years. I was hitting a wall and freezing up inside. What do we do when our computers freeze or malfunction? My technically astute, "daughter-in-chief," Rebekah reminds me to unplug. Almost two years ago I had to unplug myself from the expectations of others. A resounding, "No, I'm done. I resign. This has to stop. I am not the adapter plug, the translator, the fixer, the communicator-in-chief, the acceptor or transformer of everyone else's emotions, opinions, reactions, behaviors." How dare a mother unplug? She has no right! How dare a caring pastor unplug herself? Needs are like ocean tides coming in constantly. Can the sand retreat from the ocean floor or unplug from the rhythmic caresses and raging waves? Where can she hide?

God whispers... "Be not afraid. I go before you always. Come follow me and I will give you rest."[21] This excerpt from the song, "Be Not Afraid," became a life

---

[21] "Be Not Afraid," song sung by Elisabeth von Trapp on her CD, *"Love Never Ends."* (Sacred Sounds, Von Trapp Music), 2005.

raft for me. During our Gifts of Women worship service in 2019, a group of young women performed a liturgical dance to this song. Whenever I am feeling alone, I play the whole CD in the privacy of my home.

"Really, God? Did you say rest? Not another storm? Not another task? Not another expectation?"

"Yes."

"How do I know this is God speaking? Can you identify yourself? Isn't this Sabbath rest concept selfish and narcissistic?"

"I am speaking through your own body and your inner voice, through the longings of your heart, through medical professionals, spiritual directors and friends, through your writings, but you have to take the leap of trust – into my open arms of love, grace and total acceptance. It's a new way of connecting to the living water you are thirsty to drink. It's the only way to upgrade your spiritual software. It's the only way.... JUMP, Sue!!!"[22]

Questions for Reflection:

➢ *When in your life have you been encouraged to "unplug"?*

➢ *What brought you to the point of surrender?*

---

[22] God's voice within me.

Chapter Two

Class IV Rapids, Diving into Depression

Up until now, I have named and described many places, where my family and I have traveled and lived. This chapter acknowledges a scary inner room, where I have felt alone and trapped. I have longed for, and even begged God, and those whom I love and trust, to provide relief, companionship, empathy and understanding. I appreciate each member of my family for staying with me through this season they might want to call, "Fragile Momma" or "Angry Wife." I have been crying for help for several years. No one wants an angry or depressed pastor either; therefore, my family has borne the brunt of my illness. This season of complicated grief took a toll on all of us.

I give thanks to God for every doctor and counselor who has given me his or her focused and undivided attention, as well as professional and personal wisdom to help me navigate, what I consider a Class IV Rapids in my life. Only by looking at the turbulence of depression in the rearview mirror, can I call this period in my life God's mercy in disguise.[23]

---

[23] Excerpt from the song, "Blessings," by Laura Story, from her album, *Blessings,* (London, England: Berwick Lane Studios), 2011.

Having completed the First Health Mindfulness Based Stress Reduction program in 2013, I have been invited to participate in two, day-long retreats, one in the fall and one in the spring at the Clara McLean house every year. On November 4, 2017, I attended the day of Quiet Meditation and will record some excerpts of my thoughts and feelings on that day. The pace of the Hudson family for many years has been breathless and emotionally demanding, with very little opportunity to slow down, rest and play. As you read the words that follow, you will feel like you are moving at a slower pace, in contrast to what you have read so far.

We were invited to journal and practice many forms of meditation. Here are some excerpts of my thoughts/feelings during this time of profound depression, when I slowed down and honored my own body, mind and spirit.

> "What I want to remember about this day is the luxurious time and space of being present to myself. I loved walking barefoot on the cool grass along the edge of the healing garden. In the 'Body Scan Meditation,' my feet were elevated on the pillow and did not touch the ground at all, which felt good, because it gave my feet a break from holding the rest of my body. While walking, my feet, not my brain, were leading me. Because the grass was thick, my feet and toes sunk in deeply and one foot might sink deeper than the other. The slower I went, the less wobbly I was.

I stopped to see and honor each different type of flower and enjoyed seeing a pair of yellow butterflies playing like children in the air. Birds sang and swooped from one tree branch to another. All of creation was speaking its language of silence and song. Squishing in the luscious grass felt like a foot massage. I was surprised when the bell rang. I had savored every step.

Eating meditation was also luxurious! I used most of the hour to eat a twelve-grain sunflower-butter sandwich and a Tupperware container of vanilla bean yogurt with thawing blueberries. As I licked each spoonful and allowed each blueberry to be squeezed by my tongue and teeth, no two blueberries were the same. One lacked sweetness, several were slightly frozen, other large ones burst open in my mouth."

One of the principles of Mindfulness/Meditation is to live in the present moment, whatever it is. It also invites us to let go of what we cannot control. God is inviting me to let go right now. Elizabeth Manley, the leader of the Mindfulness program, explained the Buddhist concept of inevitable and avoidable suffering. She said that avoidable suffering occurs when we are "grasping for something we do not have" or "failing to accept what is the state of things." I have been grasping for something I do not have and it has created suffering in my life, which has led to serious, unremitting depression. Letting go is easier said than done, but offers incredible freedom, liberation and joy when we are able to embody that principle.

I have had to let go of many things, places and people in my life and recognize that letting go is the bridge to freedom and the doorway to a great adventure. In this latest experience of holding on too tightly, I find myself thrown out of my raft in a Class IV rapids, but I also know instinctively what to do. My life jacket is already on, because I wear it, whenever I get in my raft on open water. It is the life jacket of trust. I know to let go of trying, because the currents and rocks are bigger than I am. I put my feet facing downstream, lay out on my back with my head looking up to God, as I navigate through the rapids, my feet bouncing off large rocks until the next quiet pool of water will allow me to swim to the side of the river and get back in my raft. On a recent raft trip on the Nantahala River, an experienced guide rode in our raft and knew the river like the back of his hand. I trusted him one hundred percent. I now translate that trust to God, my guide for life.

Since 2008, when I identified with the hemorrhaging woman while in Bangladesh, I have been seeking God's rest and restoration, but the burdens and demands of pastoral ministry do not take a vacation. When David and I returned to Bethesda in April 2016, the expectations were off the charts for us to bring healing and restoration to a congregation that had gone through some years of discord, under the leadership of a previous pastor. The church was divided about how to respond and eventually asked the pastor to leave. As happens in these situations, there were people who were friends of the pastor and his family who left the church in anger.

I felt the intensity of peoples' expectations, and also appreciated the loving embrace with which we were received by the congregation. Rebekah and I took a much-needed vacation to New York City for my birthday right before David and I moved back to Aberdeen. We saw "Lion King" and also "Wicked" on Broadway and relished our time of rest and refreshment. When we returned, David and I were in full-scale moving mode.

After our return to Bethesda, I was trying to finish up my classes for the Spiritual Formation Certificate and decided to take the last two during the fall of 2016. Dad was still alive at the time. One of those classes was about "Sabbath." It opened my eyes to God's desire for all of God's children to practice Sabbath regularly. It is the fourth commandment and the longest of the ten. I returned from the class, taught at Montreat Conference Center, hoping and praying that I would be able to experience Sabbath rest, as a regular rhythm in our lives and ministry.

A month later I attended a Desert Pilgrimage to the Southwest as my final course for the Spiritual Formation program. It was a twelve-day pilgrimage. We stayed in a small home on Ghost Ranch, called Casa del Sol, "House of the Sun." The night before I left for the trip, I was called into dad's nursing home with the news that he was starting to aspirate. I got up early the next morning to talk to the doctor about whether or not I should cancel out of the pilgrimage. The doctor made no promises. I asked the doctor to call in Hospice while I was away. David encouraged me to go ahead on the pilgrimage, knowing that he would be here, and I could get home in a day if I needed to do that. I went on the pilgrimage, acutely aware that dad's time was limited.

When I returned, dad was stable. While on the pilgrimage I had felt God's whispers of inner assurance that my dad would pass away at a time when I would be best able to handle it. I had some fears that dad would die when I was emotionally unable to cope, remembering what had occurred when David's mother died, while we were in St. Pauls. Watching dad deteriorate took its toll on me.

When I returned home from the Desert Pilgrimage a few days after the 2016 presidential election, it was extremely difficult for me to return to the life I had left. The political climate was extremely deflating, my dad was declining and I felt like a horse refusing to jump at a Hunter and Jumper event. I did not want to re-enter a work world that was 24/7. I choked. My depression reasserted itself and from that day forward my life became a roller coaster of tears, medication, counseling appointments and increasing anger. I could no longer over-ride my own emotions to consistently do the work of ministry, but I tried my best and soldiered on for another year and a half before I had the courage and conviction to say, "Enough."

God spoke to me through creative artwork, through counselors, doctors, friends, relatives, and reading during that year and a half, but the straw that broke my back was the fact that I exploded in anger right before Christmas 2017, the first Christmas after dad passed away. Sue was not okay. In fact, I was having the closest thing I have ever experienced to a nervous break-down. The consequences of that melt-down were almost unbearable, because the people I hurt when I erupted volcanically, were the people I love the most.

Six months later, I finally leapt off my precipice of fear – which was to ask for what I needed. Why is that so difficult, especially for women? After several breakdowns, because I felt that I would be disappointing the person I love most in the world, David, my partner in life and my partner in ministry, I asked him if he would still love me if I asked for a leave of absence. He said, "Yes." Then I had to ask the Personnel Committee and the governing body of the church for a leave of absence, which would accrue from vacation days, sick days and continuing education days. The gracious response of the board was beyond my imagination. They granted me two months' leave with full pay and benefits. They wanted what was best for me. Two months of gracious space felt luxurious. Why was it so difficult to ask for what I need? I still can't answer that question; however, I believe the dive into depression jarred loose the stuck door into Sabbath, which in the original Hebrew is spelled: "YINNÁPHASH."

Questions for Reflection:

> ➤ *When have you felt like you were at the end of your rope?*

> ➤ *How have you learned to create a healthy rhythm, balancing both your work and your life?*

Chapter Three:

Place of Rest....
"YINNÁPHASH"

*W*hile studying Sabbath under Ryan Bonfiglio at Montreat Conference Center, we immersed ourselves in the Hebrew Scriptures about what Sabbath means and how we can experience it in the fast-paced world in which we are living. In Exodus 31:17 we are reminded that God practiced Sabbath while creating the world, because Sabbath is God's divine rhythm of life. "It [Sabbath] is a sign forever between me and the people of Israel that in six days the Lord made heaven and earth, and on the seventh day, God rested and was refreshed."

Since we are created in God's image, the rhythm of Sabbath is integral to our staying healthy and faithful. The Hebrew word, which means "refreshed," is "YINNÁPHASH." Although I had studied Hebrew, I did not remember that particular word, but I love its alliteration! Ryan said it is derived from the word for "soul." It means refreshed and "re-souled." We also learned that the people of Israel viewed the Sabbath as a day when they were "double-souled." I cannot fully fathom what that means, but it felt like a spring of freshwater bubbling up within me, as we practiced a traditional Jewish Sabbath, lighting the candles, resting and allowing God to re-soul us. I imagined, while Ryan was teaching, that I would love to start a "YINNÁPHASH" small group of Christian seekers, who want to be re-souled and refreshed on a regular basis!

This two-month leave of absence from ministry was God's gift of "YINNÁPHASH" to me. My hope and prayer afterward was that I could integrate the practice of Sabbath refreshment when I returned to ministry. I wanted to share this spiritual oasis and practice with others who also may be hungering and thirsting for it as they give themselves self-sacrificially to others.

Questions for Reflection:

> ➤ *What does a "Sabbath" look like in your life, or are all the days in your life the same, driven by the work you do?*

> ➤ *Where do you go and what do you do to find rest, refreshment and re-creation by God's Spirit?*

Flying Free at the Wild Goose Festival

*W*hile on my leave of absence, I attended the "Wild Goose Festival" in Hot Springs, NC, as a place where I could deepen my roots and spread my wings. I experienced three days and nights of spiritual succor and connected with people I did not know, but I felt like they were members of my tribe. I booked an Airbnb, called "Leslie's Quiet Place." The thirty-minute commute to Hot Springs included a steep gravel driveway and two miles of gravel road winding around the mountain. The local Christian radio station from Asheville came through loud and clear, even though I often lost my GPS signal on my phone.

Some of the headliners at the Festival were Barbara Brown Taylor, Brian McLaren, Doug Padgett and Amy Grant to name just a few. The Conference Brochure/ Guide was one hundred and forty pages, describing twenty-seven different venues with speakers and workshops, including about three hundred and forty-eight co-creators, who facilitated one or more of the four hundred and forty events offered at the event. Needless to say, it was hard to pick and choose where to go, but I relaxed and let God's Spirit lead me. With their emphasis on: "Spirit... Justice... Music... Art," people came and went, often sharing deeply about their experiences with people they had never met.

I spoke deeply with an African American seminary student from Atlanta, beginning her last year at Pittsburgh Seminary and I offered to pray for her this year as she discerned God's call. I also spoke deeply with a Hispanic/Latina intern at Sojourners Magazine in Washington, D.C., who was afraid to tell her pastor father where she was spending the week.

By the river, I met a man who works at the Charlotte Spirituality Center as a Spiritual Director with a specialty in Mindfulness. He aspires to be a collaborator and instrument of God's love. He was born and raised in Sri Lanka and calls himself a Devotional Non-Dualist. Whenever we bumped into each other as the Festival progressed, we spoke by name and promised to support one another on our spiritual journeys! Those are just a few of the special people who crossed my path.

Three practical workshops touched me: "Deep Listening," "Talking Circles" and "Free Verse Poetry," which I attended on Saturday. Since Friday was like drinking from a firehose, Saturday morning I was tired and had already received so much to ponder, that I asked God to walk me a little more slowly through the day. Having gone to the Festival alone, I was free to come and go, eat or drink, participate, or contemplate without having to coordinate my plans with anyone else. That was liberating, but also lonely at moments.

As I slowed my pace, I was visited by a butterfly while standing in line at the porta-potty! She landed on my wrist and stayed with me, while I took photos of her with my cell phone. When it was my turn, she accompanied me into the porta-potty. I didn't want to brush her off, because I felt she had been sent to me and was a wink from God that I was not alone. I did brush her off and she clung to the side of the porta-potty, spreading her wings. When I finished and opened the door, she flew away.

Later that day, I attended the Free Verse Poetry workshop and was asked to draw a picture of a "body" of some sort, which expressed my emotion. We drew figures and then created a poem about our embodied emotion.

What shape
speaks to me?

A butterfly rested
on my wrist
today.

She chose me
and lingered long.

When I blew
on her, she
opened her wings,
fully spread,
beautiful...

Why did she
choose me?

Now I am
choosing her as my muse
for writing my story.

She is looking
sideways with
human eyes and eyebrows

She is trying to focus,
smiling with anticipation.

A butterfly
with rosebud shaped lips,
even lipstick.
How silly! How playful!
Heart-shaped
she loves freely
and joyfully.

Twirling designs
on her wings
invite me to dance into
greater freedom
and playfulness.

"Let's fly!"
She whispers.
"Will you show me how?"
I reply timidly.

Spread your wings
and let the air
beneath your wings,
that feminine
Spirit of God,
your wild goose,
do the lifting.

Breathe her in and
set her free...
and she will set you free.[24]

---

[24] Sue Hudson, Wild Goose Conference, July 14, 2018.

Saturday unfolded like a butterfly emerging from her cocoon. The weariness lifted from my shoulders as I went from one workshop or worship experience to another. In the early evening I took a plunge in the river with a strong current. I leapt from a rope hanging over the river and perched myself on solid rock as the current caressed me and cooled me from the heat of the afternoon. Two other adventurers were in the river with me. Later, a baby copperhead snake slithered into the woods nearby. God whispered in my ear: "YINNÁPHASH." May all of God's creation breathe and rest!

Questions for Reflection:

> ➤ *When have you given yourself permission to find rest, refreshment, unwinding and healing?*

> ➤ *What shape or form in God's creation calls out to you? For me, it was a butterfly, but sometimes I am drawn to the playfulness and depth of a dolphin.*

Chapter Five:

Praying with Colors

What is the story within the stories of our lives? How do we listen to that inner voice? The following chapters will delve more deeply into how God has spoken to me by praying with colors. I did not know how to take more time to listen to my own life. How could I dive beneath the surface, when I was always moving at such a hectic pace? What if God's wisdom was waiting beneath the surface, but would require me to slow down, get some air tanks on my back and dive deeper?

Beginning in September 2018, I began attending a series of art workshops, led by Ally Markotich,[25] who also completed the Certificate in Spiritual Formation

---

[25] Ally Markotich is passionate about kindling the creative flame that lives within each of us. She's an artist, poet and Intentional Creativity® teacher who is trained in Spiritual Formation. Ally is the creator of *Soul Kindling LLC*, a portable sanctuary designed to awaken participants to their inner well of wisdom. She invites participants to a table of spiritual practice where they connect with their sacred story, re-member their creativity and ignite fresh vision for their lives with paint, visioning and writing as the tools. Her guidance leads women and men to walk their path with renewed perspective and clearer purpose. An advocate for Red Thread circles, Ally leads regular gatherings that uplift belonging and individual voice as imperative elements of the whole. Her art has been shown at Harrington Center (Columbia Theological Seminary), Moore County Fine Arts Festival (NC/ August 2019) and Litmus Gallery (Raleigh, NC/October 2018). Ally lives with her husband, Chris, two sons and yellow lab among the pine trees of North Carolina where a stop for ice cream is always possible. You can find her art, workshops and musings at www.soulkindling.com.

at Columbia Seminary. We met at one of those classes, while I was living in St. Pauls. As an art major in college, one of the professors at Columbia invited her to respond to his class using "art" as her language, rather than writing a paper. This began an awakening of her creative heart and gifts. Ally later enrolled in an on-line program called, "Intentional Creativity," with Shiloh Sophia, and has undertaken the creation of "Soul Kindling," a website and platform for her work with art-based Spiritual Formation.

Without Ally's work and leadership, my Raft of Inner Healing would be much smaller. Through these workshops, I began to discover many stories hidden in my own life. By dabbling with paint on canvases, new lines of communication were opened between God's Spirit and my own. These art workshops arrived in my life when I was ready to receive them. Characters show up on each canvas. Ally calls the characters "muses," who are bringing us wisdom that is already present within us, if we give God time to bring the wisdom to conscious awareness. "Spirited Voyager" was the first workshop I attended. The muse who appeared on my canvas opened my eyes to my love for adventure, playfulness and the guidance of the Holy Spirit. This canvas was created during a two-day workshop. What struck me most was her joy and the beautiful colors on the canvas, since I had been wrestling with depression. She was calling me to reawaken my inner child of joy, playfulness, creativity, spontaneity and trust.

Later, during Advent, the muse who showed up on my canvas, as we reflected on the life and character of Jesus' mother, was "Firebird," whose strong energy and anger revealed deep feelings that were buried within me. Firebird helped me connect to Mary, Jesus' mother, in the Bible, whose challenges as an unwed mother are often overlooked by Christians. Mary immediately withdrew after the angel's annunciation, to spend time with her cousin, Elizabeth, who was also carrying a child believed to be a gift from God. Certainly, both Mary's and Joseph's reputations were criticized when she became pregnant before God's prophecies were fulfilled. An unwed mother in Mary's time would have been shamed, even condemned to death. Joseph was tempted to "put her away quietly" until an angel spoke to him also.

The workshop, "Living from the Inside Out," showed me how to trust God's feminine voice within me. One of my friends once told me that my middle name was "adaptable," because of my ability to adjust to new cultures and to move so many times, allowing each new setting and group of people to shape me along the way. In that sense, I have spent a great deal of time as an adult serving others and letting what is "outside of me" determine what I was called to do. The culture, my loved ones, and jobs have called the shots, set the stage, and written the scripts of my life. I have allowed this, because I love to please the people closest to me, and I was strongly encouraged by my church family to pour myself out in love for others, while expecting nothing for myself. I was also raised by a mother who did that for me and the ones she loved. The symbol of the heart, the waterslide, and the smiling mouth at the center of this painting is calling me to let my inner voice lead, rather than the voices and expectations of others, who are outside of me.

I will give you a brief introduction to the muses who followed Spirited Voyager and Firebird but will dive in a little deeper in later chapters, where you will be able to view each painting and listen to the voice of each muse. "Body Embrace: Loving the Skin I Am In" was a workshop that planted seeds of new life within me, as if I was re-birthing myself, with God's help, into a new chapter of my life.

"Bursting Forth" was the name of my muse who emerged at a workshop at the Trinity Center, co-directed by Monica Hix and Ally Markotich, both graduates of the program at Columbia. "Bursting Forth" was awakening me to abundance. My "Medicine Basket" painting contains the gifts God has given me to share with the world. At the "Cultivator" workshop, which Ally facilitated at a Yoga studio, I created the most profound of all the paintings. That Muse turned out to be my maternal grandmother, who died before I was born, but who appeared on my canvas to send me a message from heaven.

"Omega," a sassy little muse, emerged during a workshop called, "Activator." She looks like she is shaking her finger and challenging me to finish writing my story, which I am trying to do right now. "Seeking Discernment" showed me that the path to wholeness would take me through a deep darkness and encouraged me to close my eyes, trust God and take the next step. "Breaking Free" portrays the butterfly emerging from her cocoon. The last two workshops of awakening were called, a "Vision Book," and "I Am." These paintings are pointing in the distance to the next steps God is inviting me to take, as our future together unfolds.

Questions for Reflection:

➤ *What resources, tools, art supplies, or creative practices have helped you tap into your inner voice of wisdom?*

➤ *What are you longing to hear or experience in your life right now?*

Chapter Six:

Spirited Voyager Shows Up

Spirited Voyager

*H*ow does this process of praying through art actually work? There is a layered process of listening to poetry prompts, imaginatively visualizing images with our eyes closed, and the choosing of colors and words, which come to our minds through verbal prompts that Ally gives us. Spirited Voyager began in this way. Ally invited us to look out on the waters of our imagination, where someone was waving to us. My muse waved to me from a simple sailboat and called out, "It's safe. Come on out. I see you." The wind was blowing on my face. She reminded me that the wind would give me the momentum I needed. She encouraged me to trust that the breath of God's wind will take me where I need to go.

On a rather huge canvas, I was reflecting on transitions. For me, it meant taking me in all of my humanness, back into a pastoral role and re-entering my family relationships. It is not always pretty – the blending of colors on the canvas. I chose red, yellow, blue and aqua. I love red on its own, but on the canvas, it looked strong and domineering. Sometimes it bleeds and disturbs the peace of the canvas.

I notice the ebbing tide, as we did some more visualizing meditations. Every cycle has its purpose. The sea's withdrawal reveals the delights beneath the surface. What is she giving me when the tide withdraws? It is exactly what I need for the journey. We are both in the boat together now. She hands me a starfish, a dolphin and a sunset. Sometimes feeling everyone's feelings can be overwhelming. She is telling me to claim the new place in my life. What needs to be integrated into your life for this transition? What are you claiming for yourself?

Patience is something I do not like to ask for, but I believe it is the gift I need. What does patience look like? Is there a metaphor for patience that I can put on the canvas? Is it a seed? A growing plant? The plant is joy, the seed is small, and it takes time to grow. I claim for myself time and space for seeds to grow, take root, and break through the soil. I claim for myself consistency and a sustainable routine, which I will create. It will be my routine, not someone else's. My pace and my space will be full of grace. It will be a lifeline to the heart of God, allowing me to breathe deeply, regularly, as it nurtures patience and fertilizes the journey ahead of me.

Patience, with her deep roots, is sturdy. She is planted, but invisible, even transparent. She does not call attention to herself. It is easier to see what she is not. She is not explosive anger or reactive departure. What would a tree of patience look like? What kind of flower or fruit would she bear? Would she be the opposite of impatiens? You can laugh now. The flowers which are called, impatiens, were named because of their impulsive response to being touched! Patience is also not a sunflower; sunflowers are too bright and smiley! Patience is more like an African violet...small, steady, enduring. She doesn't draw attention to herself.

Patience is becoming extinct in our culture. She is being choked out by speed and technology. She is a rare virtue, rarely applauded or rewarded for her steadiness. Patience holds her tongue and refuses to blame others or heap guilt on the guilty. She is modest and does not need to be right. She reveres goodness and compassion and listens without interrupting.

Patience makes eye contact...smiles...nods with understanding, affirms, or withholds affirmation if the Spirit silences her for the good of the other. Patience never shames or preaches. She can choose silence not to hurt anyone, making space in the conversation for others. Here is what my Muse wanted to tell me on that day.

"Dear Sue,

I am your Spirited Voyager,[26] inviting you into fullness of life and into life-transforming joy. Our life in Christ is always on turbulent seas, but God has given you the gifts and resources to transform the journey into a dance on the water. The sensitive starfish is only revealed when the tides ebb; she invites you to own your feelings and honor them. The social dolphin invites you into the depths where life is deep, playful and connected to your community. You also have a simple outline of the dove – the Spirit of Jesus – the one who leads you and names you, beloved daughter."

I responded, "Thank you, Spirited Voyager, will you return me to my family and church with the glow of the life beyond death, past fear? I seek that peace which passes all human understanding. I know you have

---

[26] "Spirited Voyager" was the name of the first art workshop I attended, and I asked Ally's permission to use the phrase as part of the title for my book.

been with me since the beginning of this journey. Help me to see and interpret my story through your eyes."

Questions for Reflection:

> *If you could design a two-day excursion with God, where would you go?*

> *What are three "gifts" God wants to give you for this journey?*

Chapter Seven:

Mary, Mother Lover's Wisdom

Firebird

A few months later, I attended an Advent Workshop at Bethesda, where we were invited to remember and meditate on Mary's experience of being chosen by God to give birth to Jesus. The event began with a poem by Clarissa Estes, entitled: "Untie the Strong Woman."[27] It seems that we often picture and imagine Mary as a demure woman. Estes suggests she is instead: "fire!" She is ever in motion, full of emotion, even commotion.

Where am I in Mary's story? The piece of Mary's story that attracts me in this time of meditation, is the fact that accepting God's gift and trusting God's promise of what God is doing and birthing in me has brought me some condemnation from the people I love the most. As Mary went to Elizabeth for support, I have had to find a supportive community, which has nurtured me, so that I would not let peoples' condemnation deter me from listening to God's voice in my life. Mary retreated to the home of Elizabeth, also pregnant with one of God's chosen, so that together they could welcome the new thing God was doing in their lives, which stretched both of them out of their comfort zones.

During our guided meditation, these are the notes I took in my journal. "Where am I? On my 'ocean couch' or in my outside pool, which right now is covered over for the winter. Mother Mary flies in to greet me on her God-wings. She is deep in the water with me; she is a mermaid. I jump off my float of meditation. We hold hands and dance in the water together. We go down to the deepest spot, near the drain, and do hand signals,

---

[27] Clarissa Pinkola Esteés, *Untie the Strong Woman: Blessed Mother's Immaculate Love for the Wild Soul.*(Sounds True, 2013).

body movements, and facial expressions, because we cannot speak underwater.

Mother Mary is holding my hands. She has, in her cupped hands, wings for me. She presses them into my heart and massages my heart with warmth and tenderness. "Fly!" she sings to me. As she whispers, she is urging me to fly through the seas of my life, whether calm waters or stormy ones. She is breathing "Spirit Air." What is Mary saying to me?

Dear Sue

"The depths are calling to you, Sue, do not be afraid of where that leads you: whether to the depths of the deepest ocean or into the sky's furthest horizons. I have you, Sue! I am also Mary, your mother in heaven, whose blonde bouncy hair is now yours. She and I are breathing into that heart-shaped oxygen tank that senses the depth or height, where you are traveling. There is no place you will go without us. As I stayed by my son on his darkest day, I will also be with you. As I rejoice with him now (and with Mary and Ray!), we await you with garlands of JOY!!"

Mother Mary is gently fierce and fiercely gentle. She gives me road signs along the way as I journey forward. She gives me visibility when needed, as well as invisibility when needed. For me, my Mother Lover's name is Firebird!

Questions for Reflection:

> ➢ *If verbalizing our anger in a safe space is an important part of the healing process, where has it been safe for you to share your anger or frustration without condemnation?*

> ➢ *If denying or repressing our anger and fear only makes them worse, what are appropriate ways to express and process strong emotions in our lives?*

Chapter Eight:

Living from the Inside Out

Living from the Inside Out

oy is an Inside Job, by Don Blanding,[28] was a book my mother loved. As I participated in an art workshop, entitled "Living from the Inside Out," I found myself at home in the depths of my heart. I must trust what God is doing and give the gift of listening, which I have always given freely to others, to myself. I must be still and listen to God's voice within me. What makes my eyes light up with joy? I see a water slide of thriving. A letter is in my box from "Laughing." What is the symbol on that paper? It is a water slide with a smile of delight, a heart and a shining star. I want to learn to live organically from the inside out, rather than unconsciously trying to meet the expectations of others!

Questions for Reflection:

> ➤ *Since at an early age, we learn to obey parents and teachers in order to receive love, affirmation, good grades, or other rewards; where and how do we learn to live lives of integrity without dependence on, or addiction to, external praise or rewards?*

> ➤ *Which people and what activities bring out the best in you? What is the legacy you would like to be remembered for?*

---

[28] Don Blanding, *Joy is an Inside Job.* (New York: Dodd, Mead & Company), 1953.

Chapter Nine:

Body Embrace, Loving the Skin You Are In!

Midwife to Life

 bout a month later, Ally offered the workshop, "Body Embrace, Loving the Skin You Are In." I did some intentional reflection about the fact that we must love ourselves first, in order to guide others on a healthy journey of self-care. Jesus invites us to love our neighbors as we love ourselves, not vice versa. We must be deeply connected to the living water of Jesus Christ, who never runs dry, by taking care of ourselves, so that we will be able to love others in a healthy way.

The workshop leader asked us, "What is a story or belief that is no longer working for you?" For me, the answer to that question was the premise that the Christian faith has taught me: Always put yourself last, for the last shall be first. Take up your cross and follow Jesus. I have lived into that value for most of my adult life. I was hitting a wall in Bangladesh, when I discovered that I was the hemorrhaging woman in the Bible story.

This Muse invites me to be the midwife of my own life. She invites me to hold what is deepest inside of me: my heart, my emotions, organs of life and creation, and allow that part of myself to be grounded in the earth, trees, seaweed, coral, fire, volcanic energy and God. She tells me that my body is a flowing river of life: swirling, still, curving, as the ground changes around me. Seeds of life are within me. Hold your heart and womb with quietness and strength. Be you, rarely symmetrical, but deeply centered in God's love. You are flowing, and you are at peace.

She tells me that I love pink and glow in that color. I also love blue, the color of water, which flows through and around me. These are the colors of newborn baby blankets. She tells me I am beautiful, bubbly and blessed. She challenges me to be one who helps birth others.

Questions for Reflection:

➢ *How can you treat your own body, mind and spirit with greater respect?*

➢ *What seeds are being planted in you, that you would like to nurture and tend?*

Chapter Ten:

Mothering Myself

Bursting Forth

I traveled with a few friends from Bethesda and else-where, to a weekend retreat at Trinity Center in Emerald Isle, where we were asked several questions. "Where are our mothering energies focused? Why were we drawn to this retreat?" The feminine breath of God (in Hebrew: "ruach") led me there. What gift did I bring? Germinating within me are seeds of creativity. According to Anne Lamott, as reported in the Marin Independent Journal on May 7, 2010: "We all have a quilt of mothers." What was my experience of being mothered? I remember my mom talking on the phone a lot to her girlfriends, laughing and sharing details of their days. My mom wrote a poem once about a conversation we had. She was telling me that I would understand something, "when I grew up." I put my hands on my hips, looked up at her and said, "Why don't you grow down for a change?"

I have learned that I am a deeply emotional human being. Yet, I never saw my mom cry except at her sister's burial. We were in the limousine sitting beside each other and one of her tears dropped onto my face. My mom and I shared deeply with one another on a regular basis, but I was the "crier." Mom was a stress absorber. When she was in a room, everyone else felt better. Dad was a leaf blower and managed not to take into himself the needs and emotions of others.

In my journal, I was asked to draw a picture of the "womb" that held us. The picture I drew was a cross with the following words inscribed inside it: catering to family, loving too much, people-pleasing, "should-ing" on oneself. In a moment of profound anger, I remember shouting at my mother: "Speak up to Dad! Tell him how you really feel!" I see her in me. Mom was a mid-wife of life for others, but who was her midwife when the going got tough for her? Perhaps those telephone conversations with friends were life-saving. For others, Mom was a heart full of love, laughter, joy, forgiveness, empathy, dancing, poetry, communication, deep friendships, writing, and simplicity.

We learned at the retreat about the Mother's Letter Project, initiated by a husband and wife in 2008, when they agreed to create presents for each other instead of buying gifts and then donating the difference to help others. The husband decided to collect a series of open letters from mothers to mothers, inviting people to share their stories—no matter how raw or difficult—as a way of sharing their wisdom. The husband compiled the letters in a Christmas book for his wife. Inspired by that couple, this is my letter to me:

Dear Mother Sue,

I invite me to relax the death grip of perfection and my addiction to the approval of others. Be the mother I am. It's organic. Embrace the free range of my life. Find the still point, the center of myself, the womb, where God's Spirit dwells within me. God is attached to me and meets me in love. God hugs me. The God who holds me is delightful, alive, and fun. God surrounds me with bright light and stands guard around my heart and my womb, so that I can take the creative risk, that is required of me. I am opening myself to risk everything, to trust God implicitly. Flow.

Pause. God is flowing through me, as I
rest, nurture, and feed my soul!

"Hallowing"—the hole in the center of the canvas
represents death and becomes the hollowed-out womb
for new life. God's seasons and landscapes are mir-
rored in our souls. It is the season of fall right now in
the physical world and also in my soul. It is time for
me to let go and lay fallow. It is a time of barrenness,
darkness, the slowing of my pace, the surrender of
dreams. It is painful and full of grief. The past is not
coming back. It is a time of dryness.

In Hebrew, the word for womb is "rahem," which also
means compassion and mercy. The womb is the cave
of pure creativity, where we are the creators. What is
the dying I am being called to, in order to create space
for new life? What are the gifts and delights of letting
go and releasing? I am not responsible for anyone else
right now but myself. Letting go has been a part of
my journey; it's a muscle I have used many times. It
is freeing, liberating and grounded in trust that God
holds me and the ones I love. It is the opposite of fear.
I am letting go of being transient. A woman needs a
place to go to dissolve, compost, lie fallow.

Howard W. Thurman talked about fallow times of
the spirit,[29] which have been recognized throughout
creation, since ancient times as far back as 6,000 B.C.
The fields get drained. Think of the dust bowl, when
bugs arrive in droves. People rotate crops because
nutrients are sucked out of the soil, which needs to

---

[29] Howard Thurman, "Lying Fallow," from *Disciplines of the Spirit*
(Richmond, Indiana, Friends United Press), 1977.

breathe and live wild for a while, in order to restore the soil's fertility.

As I meditate on my periods of fallowness (few and far between), I lean into God's feminine Spirit, whose wings lift me up and hold me. I nest in her arms, trusting her and yearning for her to free me to fly. I visualize myself in a warm and secure nest of God's nurturing Spirit, who tends me to wholeness.

God planted me in my mother's womb. I have grown and thrived, bloomed and lay fallow. The fruit of joy is blossoming, along with the flower of delight, whose leaves of playfulness are whispering in the wind. Red-breasted robins sit on my branches and sing freely. God is birthing my affirmation of myself and my innate creativity. Am I nurturing this unnamed newness? What do I need from God to midwife this birthing? I need focus and permission to tell the story. My baby has had many names and has been writing itself for several years. I think I am now being called to push.

Walking the labyrinth at this Mothering Retreat, I converse with my creator. "Lord, please grant me peace, as I release the past year and a half of discord, dissonance and depression. Help me to love what is." God answers: "Sue, accept that those you love the most cannot heal you. Release your grip on them, Sue, even your need for them. You are enough. Be you. Push to completion. The story has to come out!" Thank you, William Faulkner, for the words on the front of my journal, which say "If a story is in you, it has to come out."[30] Do not listen to your inner critic; complete the

---

[30] *William Faulkner Quotes for Writers about Writing,* by Robert Lee Brewer in *Writer's Digest,* Sept. 12, 2019.

job! No more condemnation or self-doubt. Release it all. Organize, edit and submit it.

As I walk into the center of the labyrinth, I feel lighter. I am twirling and free as I release it all. Thank you, Trinity Center, for your three playful dolphins on your logo, engaging each other in the heart of God: nuzzling, snuggling, leaping. It is time to integrate the task at hand. What will the book be named? Kneading Grace? Hermana de Cristo? Grace Bursting Forth? The artwork for this weekend is "Bursting Forth." She follows Spirited Voyager, Firebird, Mid-Wife to Life, and is the next season of the spirit's organic growth within me. To God be the glory, as this feminine spirit massages my being with grace.

We were invited to look at our Muse's bowl on the canvas. What do I see in my Muse's bowl? I see a tongue of fire. It is on fire, but not being consumed or destroyed by the fire. It has red stripes. Perhaps I am resistant to the black hole in the center where her heart is. There are vines around her. She is covered, surrounded, connected to her sisters on this retreat. I am not uprooted; I am planted.

What does the dark hole represent? It is the emptying of the small ego, which fears exposure, vulnerability, and being fully known and available to Christ in me. The red stripes of hardship are blood-stained, limited, held back, but now they do not hold me. I am free, but the marks are there, like Jesus' nail-pierced hands. But now the stripes are beautiful, blessings in disguise. How shall we travel home? The dark hole in the center is the dove and my thumbs are holding it. They need to release it to experience peace.

Talk to me, Bursting Forth!

"Sweet Sue, be you. As yourself, you are a gift. Let go of the Spirit-bird in your hands from your deepest self, and let her fly free. She needs to take her first breath, this bird, this dove you are birthing, this story you are telling. Spring is "bursting forth" from you, in you; the eggs are hatching, the voices chirping, the flowers blossoming, resting on the nest of safety you are becoming for others.

Others can rest in your embracing nest to find solace, affirmation, to renew, refill. You can be a portal, a spicket of grace for others, as well as for yourself. Spray the hose of my endless love and grace back upon yourself, as the glistening drops of water sparkle in the sunlight. Nest of grace, soul on fire, be Sue; be you!! You are "fireworks."[31]

Questions for Reflection:

➤ *Why is it so hard for women to love ourselves as we are? Do men struggle with the same issues?*

➤ *How do we learn to balance healthy love for ourselves with a healthy love for others, without losing ourselves in the process?*

---

[31] Katy Perry, "Fireworks," Teenage Dream. (Trondheim, Norway: Stargate), 2010.

Chapter Eleven:

Medicine Basket

Medicine Basket

185

shorter workshop at Ally's home, "Medicine Basket," invited us to pack a basket with all of the healing gifts we bring to others. Ally asked, "What is a remedy or form of healing you would like to be known for?" What came to my mind was my bathtub, which fills the corner of my bathroom and has some jets to churn the water. I would like to be known as a "water healer." I am reminded of the simple song, "I've got a river of life flowing out of me, makes the lame to walk and the blind to see, opens prison doors, sets those captives free; I've got a river of life flowing out of me."[32] How can we be "healing pools" for others? Can a person be a space? Can we create space for grace, first, within ourselves, and then, for others?

As we meditated on these prompts, I created a medicine basket that is heart-shaped and slings over my shoulder, like a traveling bag, so that my hands can be free to hug others, since hugging is some of the medicine I offer. One former church member greeted me, as "the one who hugs." I will also bring some sparkling running water, a beautiful fan, a journal, and a pen that has multi-colored ink.

---

[32] "Spring Up, Oh Well," *Singalong 2* (Phil Wickham, VEVO), 2018.

Questions for Reflection:

> ➤ *Describe the "soul medicine" you carry within you, that people who know you and work with you, appreciate the most?*

> ➤ *What is your love language?*[33] *(words of affirmation, physical touch, quality time, gifts, or acts of service)*

---

[33] Gary Chapman, *The Five Love Languages.* (Chicago, Illinois: Northfield Publishing), 1973.

Chapter Twelve:

The Cultivator

Cultivator, my grandmother

*A*t the Cultivator Workshop, on the day after my birthday in 2019, we reflected on how transformation takes place. Macrina Wiederkehr's book, *Seven Sacred Pauses,*[34] highlights the twilight hour, which is a thin veil between heaven and earth. It is also the poet's hour, or the mystical hour, the hour of grace, where life begins. She calls it the "cosmic kiss" which consummates what it touches. It is the place between darkness and light, death and life. When a butterfly emerges from the cocoon, new life begins on wobbly wings. What areas in my life are being filled with new life? I came to this art workshop, because I have found that my soul and God can converse with each other here.

What needs purification and renewal for me? I need healing and renewal in my closest orbit. My hope and intention for this workshop is to nurture myself and hear God's voice through this experience, as a window or door of light, which will welcome greater reconciliation and harmony in my family. I am invited to doodle in my journal. I draw a heart with the word, "harmony," playfully written inside it. Outside the heart are musical notes.

Who has been an archetype or cultivator in my extended family? I think about my mother's mother, Susie Alsop Butler, as one who cultivated love. One of my mother's cousins, George Mechlin, told me that my grandmother was the person who embodied love for him, especially when his parents divorced. He was always welcome at her home and she always had plenty of food to share. I "taste" my grandmother's presence,

---

[34] Macrina Wiederkehr, *Seven Sacred Pauses: Living Mindfully Through the Hours of the Day.* (Notre Dame, Indiana: Sorin Books), 2008.

even though we have never met on this earth. From death, she dances. I taste her cooking for the first time.

When this workshop concludes, we are asked to let the person on the canvas speak to us. My grandmother dictates:

"Dear Susie, I never got to meet you or hold you in my arms, but your mother named you after me. In other words, you are the one born out of my ashes, and you are bringing into the world strength and love, which the world hungers to receive.

I didn't get the opportunity to play much. George, my husband, was an alcoholic with an incredibly tender heart. He broke our hearts when he didn't come home at night, but when he was home, we laughed and talked and loved each other.

I know you have been seeking, and you are exhausted, because the women in our family have loved deeply and often died younger than our spouses. I want you to love more wisely, attending to your own needs, playing, symbolized by the volleyball buried in the lower right corner of the canvas, which needs to rise to greater prominence.

Love is my gift to you, but it is an assertive love that my generation never knew.

We sacrificed ourselves and our health to care for others. Your mother and I are now your cheerleaders in heaven. We already have our crowns. May you take the ball through the end zone of healing, reconciliation and harmony among the different notes, chords and rhythms in our family and our world."

When I realized that my grandmother spoke words of comfort and hope from the canvas in front of me, I felt awe. It took my breath away to know that heaven had kissed me through this workshop, through someone I had heard so much about, but never encountered in person. When I shared her letter with the larger group, there was a brief moment of holy silence in the room.

Questions for Reflection:

➢ *Have you ever sensed the presence or received some communication from a relative that has already passed away?*

➢ *In your extended family, who was the person that made you feel special?*

Chapter Thirteen:

The Activator

During this period of about a year and a half of my life, I answered God's call to create at least once a month and sometimes twice. I was finally honoring my inner journey and giving myself permission to be messy, rowdy, and free to think my thoughts. I gave my full-bodied YES! I am a creative "being," not a creative "doing." Every bone in my body is creative! Ally quoted her mentor, Sophia Shiloh, from her Intentional Creativity training, saying: "We must be fierce about taking the time we need to do creative work." This workshop was designed to activate the creativity we hunger and thirst to explore, which, for me, is writing.

My definition of creativity is allowing the Spirit of God to generate newness, using whatever gifts and talents are ours to share. It is important to courageously color outside the lines and outside the box. We need to find fresh words, ideas and patterns that are colorful, unrepeatable, to bring something out of nothing.

Where is that creativity bubbling up? I feel called to write my story and trust, that if I commit to it, I will make and take the time to put pen to paper and colors on the page. I love colors: lots of reds, pinks, blues, greens, violet, and gold. On this canvas, a lady with guts is showing up and calling me out. Her name is Omega, which is the last letter of the Greek alphabet.

What do you see, Omega? I see years of life experience in Omega's face: wrinkles which deepen with her smile. She asks me: "What do your eyes see?" My answer is that I see people in their wholeness, imagining what is hidden or concealed, hungry, or desiring. "What activates and rejuvenates you?" she wonders. "Lavender scents awaken me to the depth of life, to wisdom, to integration and the gleaning of life experiences."

"What words do you desire to speak, Sue? Stand tall, sister Sue, in your Sueness. Open all the areas of your lungs. Fill them with words, as the Spirit whispers them. Spirited Voyager, it's time to board your ship, cut the ties, say a prayer and say goodbye.[35] We are ready to sail now. Your boat is putting out into deeper water."

There was a small heart at the center of the labyrinth today. The heart reminds me that it is time to complete, to finish, to fulfill. I hear words of affirmation, which call forth beauty, elegance, humility, kindness, love. Yes, my heart needs healing. As this workshop concludes, Omega speaks to me:

"The story is out in you, Sue. Breathe the words onto the pages, as you inhale and exhale. God's Spirit has breathed your story into you. Exhale what you know is there. It will be something out of nothing, the kiss of the pen to the pages. The story led you here tonight. Your hand is aflame, taking what is in your heart onto the page. Trust the unfolding vulnerability; the time will expand to be exactly what you need."

---

[35] For King and Country, "Burn the Ships," from the album, *Burn the Ships.* (Australia: Word Entertainment), 2018.

Questions for Reflection:

➤ Who has cheered you on in the last lap of a race you are running, or a task you are trying to complete?

➤ What barriers are holding you back from doing what you love the most?

Permission Box

Permission Box

On May 10, 2019 (Rebekah's birthday) I created a permission box, which allowed me to explore the ways I have given my power away to others, because I wanted to please them. Sometimes we let the opinions of those we love the most censure us from being fully ourselves. These days, I am not listening to the "No's" of people who think they know what is best for me. I am reclaiming, "Yes." People that know me well, know not to tell me, "Never." I am stubborn and strong. Be careful when that fire is burning. I am welcoming the wild stallion back. I am unlocking the gate for the wild stallion to be free in my life.

I am giving myself permission to use my time for things that are important to me: writing my book; practicing Spanish; relaxing in my swimming pool; confronting untruths, wherever they emerge; spending time to love and laugh with my children; using time as God leads me by listening to God's voice first; being a midwife for other women; being a midwife for my daughters to bloom; saying "no" to other peoples' expectations; saying "no" to my husband, children and church, when they do not understand my choices and decisions; always honoring God's timing, which allows for waiting, emptiness, and transformation.

On the inside of the permission box, there is a picture from a magazine of children playing in a make-believe tent. I am imagining Dorothy's ruby red slippers, taking me home with a whole new set of eyes. The children in the picture are laughing, dancing, loving. My permission box speaks to me:

> "Bathe in the delicious living water of God's love first, absorb the inner wisdom first, laugh at life's incongruities first, love yourself first, so that those who love you will see in you the abundant life that God describes and creates, the garden of life that God calls good, the harmony

God breathes into all whom God loves. You have permission to put back on your 'rose-colored glasses' with life in all of its abundance every single day."

Questions for Reflection:

➤ *What have you NOT given yourself permission to do in a very long time?*

➤ *When are you motivated by guilt, rather than grace?*

Chapter Fifteen:

Place of Belonging

Belonging

The next divine invitation through art asked me to reflect upon a time of isolation in my life when I did not have a place to belong. I clearly remember the experience of being alone, when we could not return to India after we had sold our home in Southern Pines. I was then asked to come up with an "adjective" that I associate with the feeling of "belonging." For me, the adjective which came to mind was "steady." Sometimes I see myself as more volatile than steady, but during this art workshop, I chose "steady" as my intention.

My place of belonging looks a bit like a sailboat, which is not grounded, because with all the moves and changes in our lives, I have not felt "steady" very often. In a sailboat, the sailor must work hard to catch the wind, by tightening and loosening the sails, as needed, then trim the sails in order to ride smoothly. My sailboat grounds itself on top of my new house in Southern Pines. A flowered cushion I purchased from Big Lots for a lounge chair in our back yard is now a resting place where I fall asleep in the warm sunlight in the back of the house. Ah, I sense that I am finally home. Recent purchases make me feel more at home here: the swing on the front porch, the glass coffee table with a canoe underneath it. Welcome home, Sue! You have arrived. This is your safe space. Though not everything is unpacked, the newness is wearing off and you are beginning to settle, here, where God has led you to be.

Your home is your safe and secure place where your artwork is welcome, your colors can bloom, where your book will be born. Your children can come here for love and grounding, where the sun shines, the rain falls and winds blow, and loved ones laugh, play and pray together. Your symbol is a sailboat grounded on a house. Trim your sails, so they don't flap too hard when the winds are howling. Take down the sails when lightning strikes. Find solace and rest in the home below the boat. You belong here. You are finally docking your boat and settling down.

Questions for Reflection:

> ➤ *Where and with whom do you feel that you belong most comfortably?*

> ➤ *What adjective would you choose to describe what belonging feels like for you?*

What is my Piece... to bring Peace?

Bridgett

*I*n August 2019, Ally and I introduced the practice of spiritual formation through creative artwork to the leadership at Bethesda Presbyterian Church. Ally facilitated the experience for the leaders who chose to attend. The elders, deacons and Sunday school teachers were invited and the workshop was funded by the Christian Education Committee. The theme of the workshop was "Claiming our Piece...to Claim our Peace."

Often spiritual leaders in a congregation feel burdened to do more work than they are called and equipped to do. Other leaders sometimes feel tasked with responsibilities that do not necessarily utilize their gifts and talents. If we all try to do everything that needs to be done, it leads to burn-out. This workshop was designed to help participants discern what might be their "piece," contribution, or offering that would contribute to the Body of Christ functioning as a whole, which leads to greater "peace" for everyone.

Ally encouraged all of us to reflect on what we feel is our unique, sacred responsibility in the life of our families, or in the life of the church. Art and meditation were designed to help us gain clarity about our unique purpose. She encouraged us to risk believing in ourselves, as we work through the experience together. Our first "red thread" question as a group was to pinpoint what most drains our energy? For me, I feel drained when people do not hear me or acknowledge me in a situation or a group of people. When I feel voiceless, or when I feel that my voice is unwelcome, it drains me.

This reminded me of an experience when I was a teenager on a Middle School Retreat with my church's youth group. Suzy, a woman who came up to me during one of the breaks, asked me if I wanted to say something. I was startled by her question, because I was shy at the time, and she "saw me," perhaps even better than I saw myself on that day. I think it brought tears to my eyes that she noticed me and wanted to know what I was thinking. I have never forgotten how good it felt to be noticed by her and invited to speak.

The second round of our red thread circle focused on the question: "What brings you peace and joy?" My answer is prayer, which I see as the intersection of heaven and earth, the place where healing occurs. I had a spiritual mentor in Seoul, Korea, when David and I served as Mission Co-workers there. She had been a career missionary with her husband. She gathered people in her home for prayer every Friday morning where we would pray for the healing of individuals, nations and the entire world. When we would talk on the phone, Vonita would often end our conversations with these words: "Well, Sue, we have talked enough about this. It is time to pray. When we bring God into our conversation, it makes all the difference in the world." Her practice of praying with me over the phone has led me to do the same when anyone asks me to pray for them. We stop and pray. As I wrote this paragraph, two people reached out to me for prayer: one by text message and one by email. I stopped and prayed for each of them.

As Ally led our visioning meditation that afternoon, she brought a cake with the word, "Peace," decorated in blue icing. At the conclusion of our time together, we served individual "pieces" of cake, which together made up the whole cake, representing the whole church and the whole world. She asked us to visualize Mary and

Jesus on a blanket beside a warm campfire. We cannot carry the whole cake to them because it is too heavy for us. What is our "piece" that we need to carry to our families, to the church, or the world? I recognized in this workshop, that I am "one who invites others" into a closer relationship with Mary and Jesus. I am "one who gathers people together."

The painting on my canvas speaks to me. Her name is Bridgett.

"Dear Sue,

What is your 'piece'? It is connection and color. You are under an arched bridge, where heaven and earth reach out and touch each other, but you do not need to bear the weight of the bridge. God has built the bridge. The heart and star of light mark the intersection where heaven kisses the earth and your role, or 'piece,' is to invite, guide, lead people to that meeting place. Through words of prayer, spoken from your heart, you guide people to that spiritual intersection where Jesus and Mary, God, the Father, Son and Holy Spirit do the rest. You point, guide, take people by the hand and lead them there, but you don't have to carry or hold up the bridge. Keep inviting people to this holy intersection of eternity and time, heaven and earth, resurrection, new life and new beginnings."

That workshop was a landmark one for me personally because I was in conversation with God about whether or not to continue working as a pastor at Bethesda. Although David and I, as a clergy couple, were both "supposed to be working part-time," according to the Presbyterian system, I was feeling the weight of the world on my shoulders in August of 2019. I came to believe that there is no such thing as a part-time ministry. That summer had been particularly full with Vacation Bible School, where I was in charge of the Bible stories every night, and a Mexico Mission trip, for which I was the leader of the team.

There were some significant challenges before, during and after both of those events. Several of the youth on the trip had phones and money stolen from their rooms at the beginning of our time in Tabasco, Mexico, where I had traveled twice before, but this was the first time something like that had occurred. There was a lot of stress on all of the adult leaders and the parents at home.

Shortly after we returned from Mexico, we also learned that our partners in Tabasco, Mexico, were planning a trip to visit Bethesda and the Presbytery in October; however, we would be hosting their visit, since the Presbytery did not have funds, and was not expecting these guests until the following year. That required me to line up homes of church members who would be willing to host our guests, as well as providing transportation to events, translators, meals and opportunities for our guests to go shopping.

During that workshop, I was trying to discern whether or not my "piece" to serve the Body of Christ would lead me to remain in the position where I was serving as a pastor, or whether I was being led into some other kind of ministry that would give me a new "piece" of the puzzle to further God's "peace" in my family and in Christ's body in the world at large.

Questions for Reflection:

> ➢ *When have you served in a leadership position when you felt "the weight of the world on your shoulders"?*

> ➢ *How do you discern what God is calling you to do in your family, church, community, or world?*

Chapter Seventeen:

A "Mappy" Quest

Discernment

*V*ery soon after the workshop experience with Bethesda's leaders, our family passed through a difficult season. David's father, Lamont, had been living in the skilled nursing unit at Sharon Towers in Charlotte. We visited him as often as we could. Rebekah was the person in our family who still lived in Charlotte, so she often stopped by to see him on her way home from work. As Labor Day was approaching, David's brothers alerted him to the fact that their dad was declining. Fortunately, all three of the brothers were with him on August 30, 2019, along with Rebekah. He was under Hospice Care for a while, but every time we visited he was able to converse and always asked questions about how the church was doing. Both Rebekah and Mary came home to Southern Pines that weekend, since they both had Monday off work. The next morning David received word from Sharon Towers that his father had passed away on Saturday morning, August 31, which was David's brother Harold's birthday.

Plans were made to have a memorial service the following weekend since both Harold and Roy had traveled to Asheville for Labor Day weekend. The brothers met later the next week to make their plans, scheduling Lamont's memorial service for the following Friday. The next weekend, I was already committed to doing a wedding rehearsal on Friday night and a wedding on Saturday afternoon, as well as being in charge of a special Rally Day Sunday School program, utilizing some of the Spiritual Formation practices we had used with the leaders earlier that month. I was also preaching and leading worship that Sunday. It was good that David's responsibilities were limited the following weekend; however, my plate was filled to overflowing. I loved David's father dearly, so Lamont's death knocked me out of my raft emotionally and left me scrambling for shore on my own, so that David and the girls could spend quality time with their siblings and cousins in Charlotte.

Later that same weekend of the memorial service, when we were eating lunch after church as a family, Rachel expressed her need and desire for me to visit her in Alabama, where she had moved that summer to take a Spanish-teaching position. She had spent the previous year in Madrid completing her Masters in Spanish through Middlebury College. Rachel's new job was stressful and demanding. She was hoping I could provide some love and support for her during her fall break, which happened to overlap with the dates of the visit from our partners from Tabasco, Mexico. There is no question that I was feeling the weight of the world on my shoulders that day. After the girls departed that afternoon, David had another memorial service to lead. I decided it was time for me to take a break and head to Roanoke, Virginia, to spend time with my sister-in-law, Robyn, where I could relax from all of the stress and reconnect with her in her new home which I had not seen yet.

In the midst of this family stress and church responsibilities, Ally led an art workshop that focused on, "The Map We Make Ourselves." She invited us to draw a door to the inside of ourselves and to trace our life's journey, noting detours, dead ends, and destinations. All of the journey was our sacred road and all of our emotions were welcome along the way. We had to look and see on our canvases, where home was, and where our journey began.

As I looked at my pilgrimage on the canvas, it was starkly divided at the center. In fact, I had traveled a huge circle, which, for me, represented the world, but I found myself back at the beginning, near the place I had begun. I was looking at the line across the center, which appeared dark and undefined. I believed I was being asked to re-enter my life at the center. Would it be a shared or solitary path? I did not know. But I was absolutely sure God was with me and calling me to trust.

The door I was invited to open on the canvas required a key that looks like a large drop of water, perhaps a "tear," through which I needed to enter this future place. The symbol of gratitude was my little, "amigo," the tree frog I had befriended in my swimming pool, who had died that morning, and was inviting me to let die what needs to die or let go of what I cannot control in my life. Amigo tells me to trust the Creator to keep re-creating.

The woman on this canvas is named the "Voice of Discernment." She speaks:

"Dear Sue,

I hear and count your tears, every single one of them, as this new day welcomes you. I claim life for you, not death. But you must first pass through the waters. They will not overwhelm you. You must balance and weave the threads of the water's edge to re-integrate and calibrate the future. It is a painful time, but will bear the fruit of these labors in God's time and God's way. You are at the center of this new future and it will integrate all of the edges, as well as the broken places in your life. You are entering a deep and silent place, but you are not alone. Trust, wait, listen, pray. I hear you; you are heard and you are loved. Your sighs too deep for words are heard, seen, understood, embraced, loved and transformed."

Questions for Reflection:

➤ *For me this time felt like a "dark night of the soul." Can you describe such a time in your life?*

➤ *Who, in addition to God, do you turn to for support when you feel overwhelmed?*

Revelation

Awaken!

$\mathscr{L}$ater in September, the "Revelation" art work-shop allowed us to invite God's mystery to reveal itself in our lives. What is luminous in us? Ally read, "Witness," a poem in *Tea with the Midnight Muse*, by

Shiloh Sophia.[36] We must be witnesses of ourselves. We must give ourselves as a love offering to our own life. Ally challenged us to draw on a piece of paper with both hands moving at the same time. She invited us to think about a time in our lives when we have received advice, which did not work. The shape that appeared on my canvas looked like the two wings of a butterfly.

The advice I receive from others is often based on pleasing the "greater good" – which is defined as the church, the community, or the preferences of key players, who exert influence and have decision-making power. Is my choice practical, convenient, financially responsible? I have had to learn that sometimes I am the only one who hears my inner voice of wisdom. Months and years later, my decision, which others question in the moment, is exactly what I needed to do and the results affirm my decision. One Spiritual Director advised me not to poll other people to find my inner wisdom, but rather to trust my inner voice. [37]

I am a writer and it's time to celebrate her identity at this time in my life's journey. The story is in me, waiting to be told. Welcome and receive this feminine author into your mind, heart, home and family relationships. Be you, Sue! Write on! You are called, chosen, affirmed and held by Her.

My canvas talks to me.

---

[36] Shiloh Sophia, "Witness," *Tea with the Midnight Muse: Invocations and Inquiries for Awakening,* (Carlsbad, CA: Balboa Press, A Division of Hay House), 2017.

[37] Dr. Martha Robbins, Professor Emeritus, Pittsburgh Theological Seminary.

"My dear butterfly, if you stretch your wings wide open, you will fly free, but you need to be centered by the inner wisdom within you, taking your guidance and lead from My Voice within you. I am yours and you are mine, butterfly. I feel the tension and pull of two wings pulling in different directions – taut and at times tangled.

Do you see the fire, which is heating up the inner wisdom, purifying and releasing it, expressing itself for the first time, winking, awakening? My name is 'Awaken!' Yes, awakening can be a bit messy. Awake, my beloved, break free and fly."

Questions for Reflection:

1) *Describe a time when you felt pulled in opposite directions, as you tried to follow God's guidance and also tried to please key people in your life?*

2) *What were the short term and long term consequences of that decision?*

Chapter Nineteen:

The Vision Book

(front and back) of the book

*I*t was not too long after that workshop that I awoke in the middle of the night and kept hearing God say to me, "October 31." It confused me at first. I wondered what God was telling me to do. When it kept happening over and over again, I realized that God wanted me to let go of the pastoral position sooner rather than later, so the rush and busyness of the holiday season would not capsize my raft again, as it had done two years earlier. The stress and demands would never cease and there is never a good time to say goodbye. I finally got the courage to tell David the date. He strongly urged me to consider waiting six months, so that we could prepare the congregation and delegate my responsibilities to others. I thought about it for several days and then said, "If God gave me the date, who am I to negotiate with God?" David agreed. However, we did not want to tell anyone about this decision, until after we had the opportunity to host the visitors from Tabasco, Mexico.

Rev. Francisco Magaña was our guest preacher from Tabasco, Mexico on October 15, with my friend, Marty Prince, a retired Spanish teacher, serving as his translator. Francisco's sermon was a perfect confirmation of my own decision. When God told Elijah, his prophet, where to hide when King Ahab was seeking to take his life,[38] the hiding place was not far from the palace. Rev. Francisco asked us: "What if Elijah had tried to negotiate with God, saying, 'But God, that does not seem like a safe enough place?' No, Elijah trusted that God was the one who knew best and would protect him if Elijah simply trusted and obeyed."

---

[38] I Kings 17:2-3

My last day of employment at Bethesda Presbyterian Church as one of their two pastors was November 10, 2019. I made this decision with great difficulty because it felt like I was being torn apart, like the butterfly wings in my painting, "Revelation." It had been my dream to return to Bethesda as a clergy couple. David and I have complementary gifts and talents. Some would say we are better together than apart. The affirmations of pastoral ministry and my love for the people and the job were great. However, listening to my soul speak through the works of art I had created, I knew that I needed to make a change in my priorities and use of time. I needed to spend more time with my children, who live in different communities. I also needed uninterrupted time to write the story, which the women on my canvases have been urging me to do. A clear message came to me from my divine source, that I needed to act sooner, rather than later. With the closing of that partnership chapter, I experienced deep grief. At the Presbytery's request, I was asked not to attend worship or any church activities for three months, with the exception of Christmas services, when I could attend with my children. Those were three agonizing months for me. At some moments, I questioned my own decision. It was an excruciatingly emotional time for our entire family.

Moving forward, Ally offered a Visioning Workshop, which was the perfect time for me to converse with God about the upcoming year. Several poems were read to bring inspiration. We were then invited to imagine in our mind's eye, where we felt most grounded. Ally invites us on an imaginative journey. "Go somewhere," which represents this new vision and calling in our lives. I pack up bags of journals, papers, poems and folders. When she asks us what form of transportation I would take, I decide on a catered airplane from the small airport in Moore County, where I hire a pilot to fly me to a retreat center, something like "Casa del Sol" (House of the Sun) at Ghost Ranch in Abiquiu, New Mexico, where people gather to hear my story. I am becoming the message I want to share.

Having navigated the rapids of Christian mission and ministry around the globe for decades, God is shifting my message. In order to love God with my whole heart, mind, soul and strength, I need to love myself fully and unconditionally first. I need to be rooted in God's rivers of unconditional love, where I am secure, grounded and re-filled continuously. For this is the organic flow of love, which brings God great joy. What has held me back from granting myself this permission? Perhaps, there has been some self-doubt; however, the larger resistance has been from the church's message of self-denial, self-sacrifice, and always putting others first. My new message of love has turned me upside down!

As we began the first quadrants of our Vision Book, Ally gave us four terms to explore: What is my passion? What legend do I want to leave? What is my dream? Who are my beloveds? First, we did a wash of two colors as a background for one side of the book. I chose red and yellow, which give the background a hot flavor.

My passion manifests itself as two swirls of green lines that indicate "depth" and "connection" to each other. The swirls connect and intersect, taking the form of a heart. Another red heart grows from the top of the swirls and contains the word, "Love." Love is, in fact, my passion. I love giving and receiving love and have traveled to many different countries and continents to share love with people of different cultures. Despite language and religious differences, I am curious to know other people deeply, understand their life stories and connect, where we can. Human beings everywhere have much in common.

This passion is rooted in my faith that God is love and we all love because God first loves us. (I John 4:19) I strongly believe that all people in the past, present and future are created by God and loved by God. While journeying as a child of God on planet earth, it is my passion and privilege to express and demonstrate love to people everywhere.

My legend is to be a "bridge," or connector of people who are different. The bridge on this quadrant represents the connection between heaven and earth, between God and human beings. As a person who "bridges," my calling or "work" is to be a person of deep prayer. I long to introduce people to their Creator and their fellow created beings, regardless of how different we might be. I find joy and pleasure in connecting people to God and each other, so that we can function in a healthy manner and respect the uniqueness of all people, practicing kindness and justice in all of our human relationships.

My legend is also connected to the quadrant of my dream. There is a large heart that overlaps these two quadrants because my "church" or "parish" is the world, which includes Christians in all of their diversity, as well as people of other faiths. The heart represents the heart of God, which contains people of many different faiths, who are seeking a deeper understanding and connection with God. I have drawn symbols to represent Jews, Hindus, Buddhists, Muslims, Taoists. I see all people as worthy, valued, loved and beautiful and I feel called to pastor in a larger community, where diverse people intersect with one another. Religious institutions tend to be places where birds of a feather flock together.

The final quadrant we created is space for our beloveds, which for me is represented by an open door. I feel called to minister and serve people who are open. My beloveds include seekers, foreigners, strangers, dreamers, courageous women, adventurers, edge dwellers, the weary, the homeless, the "others," servers, questioners, misfits, vulnerable women and men, explorers and anyone open to learn, grow, be challenged, convicted or transformed through their encounters with God and other people.

The surprise for me in this process of visioning is the fact that I have been pulling back and focusing inwardly in recent months, which some might consider selfish. However, my visioning process illuminates for me the fact that I am seeking broader exposure and want to be available to a larger community. I want to be connected to the Church with a capital "C" and the world-at-large, created and loved by God, and called according to God's purpose. Focusing more deeply is leading me to serve in a broader capacity to a community that is yet unknown to me. Every new path begins with one step. Through this process of visioning, I am creating the next few steps for the year 2020.

Questions for Reflection:

> ➤ *What is your strongest passion? What is the legend you would like to leave for the world?*

> ➤ *Who are your beloveds? How are you called to love and serve them?*

Chapter Twenty:

Who Am I?

Who Am I?

The final chapter in "The Raft of Inner Healing" will focus on who I am. The "I Am" workshop was an opportunity to integrate our inner and outer selves, which are often divided. Our deepest desire is to embody the identity God desires for us. Ally invited us to look at the division which exists within us, the paradox of our lives. As we embrace this mystery honestly, we want to narrow the gap between our inner and outer selves, the division between the "lover" and the "critic."

Who have I not been that I want to be? I want to be valued for my voice. I don't want to be silent and voiceless. My voice as speaker, pastor and writer expresses love and sees good, but when I lose my voice, I become angry and critical. When I am silenced, I erupt like a volcano.

I am also one who seeks and affirms the positives in other people. I see God's image in everyone I meet. I love to coach, mentor, and invite people to grow and flourish from the inside out. It is who I am, what I do, and how God made me. The archetype I envision is Mother Wisdom, who speaks wisdom to those who are listening. Brené Brown's book, *The Power of Vulnerability*, talks about women needing to have a strong back, soft front and wild heart![39] Mother Wisdom, I want to be your voice in this world. I want to always speak the truth with love; however, some truths are sharp. Help me to soften their impact, but not silence the truth. Mothers embody truth wrapped in love, so I need you, Mother Wisdom, to mentor me on this journey. The voice of

---

[39] Brené Brown, *The Power of Vulnerability: Teachings on Authenticity, Connection and Courage,* (Louisville, CO: Sounds True), 2012.

wisdom is not sharp or reactive, but mindful, patient and also brave beyond measure!

What three elements will I bring to this canvas to bless the integration I am seeking? I will bring the color of living water, which cleanses, purifies and satisfies our deepest thirst. My fruits are blueberries in abundance...small, not flashy, but nutritious, sweet, and enhancing the quiet flavor of vanilla ice cream. My path has led me to the place of integration where there will be no more wandering. I am home. My voice is welcome, valued and wise. I begin to grow roots, my wings are maturing. My voice is grounded and I am free to speak.

Ally invites us to write down six "who's" that I would like to grow into this year, as key ingredients to my identity. Then we are asked to write down six "descriptive" words. We shuffle both sets and then randomly match one from each set with one from the other set. I am amazed by the pairings that appear! Here is my poem, "I am..."

My name is Ocean of Wisdom,

Dalai Sophia.

I am a *bold writer*

and an *honest speaker.*

I offer *accepting love*

and extend my hand as a

warm guide,

who walks in community

towards the heart of God.

On our way
we encounter
soft truth, which is
mindful wisdom
purified.
I am integrating all the
colors and connections
of an adventurous life,
which allowed me
to touch the
corners of the earth.
I am an intimate
connector of
God's beloveds.
I hover in deep water,
at home and breathing in
God's unconditional love.

During this workshop, I gained a vision of where God is leading me into the future. My journey into the depths of my own heart and God-given spiritual desires has revealed my calling to the larger community. I am called to be a "Wellspring of Women's Wisdom" in a culture where women have been given great freedom to become all that they are intended to be, but whose voices are still silenced, side-lined, or dismissed by decision-makers in places of leadership and authority.

I have lived in countries that are much more traditional, where women's roles are more restricted, such as Pakistan and India. Yet in both countries, women have served as Prime Ministers. I look forward to the day when women will be recognized fully for their gifts, talents and unique feminine wisdom in every country on earth, because the world hungers and thirsts, as never before, for collaborative and mutually respectful leaders.

I love the church of Jesus Christ; however, I also recognize that institutional religion has been slow to trust sacred feminine voices throughout history, and has at times suppressed the words and teachings of women. The Dalai Lama apparently said: "The world will be saved by the Western women."[40] I find it intriguing that this well-beloved and respected Tibetan spiritual leader places hope in "Western women."

It was a privilege for me to teach a bright woman educator at Gujranwala Theological Seminary in Pakistan in 1996 and 1997. I later recommended her for a graduate-level degree at Louisville Presbyterian Theological Seminary, which she received and completed. Fellow students laid hands on Nosheen Khan before she returned to her country, praying for the Holy Spirit to anoint her life and ministry, knowing that the Presbyterian Church of Pakistan did not ordain women pastors. It is a joy to me that she eventually became the first ordained Presbyterian woman pastor in the Presbyterian Church of Pakistan. She was also

---

[40] The statement was made at the Vancouver Peace Summit, in September 2009, and is quoted in, *If Women Rose Rooted: A Life-Changing Journey to Authenticity and Belonging*, by Sharon Blackie, p. 19.

recognized as a Distinguished Alumni of Louisville Seminary in 2019. She presently serves as the Principal of Gujranwala Theological Seminary, where she was once my student.

As my Hispanic friend and colleague once asked me over twelve years ago, "Why does the Presbyterian Church not have 'street ministers' like St. Francis of Assisi?" Looking back through those twelve years of struggle, I see that I was indeed a spiritually hemorrhaging woman, who managed to grasp the corner of Jesus' cloak, while on pilgrimage in Bangladesh. Twelve years later, I am experiencing the Spirit's inner healing, seeing a new vision of the future, and welcoming my calling to be a "Wellspring of Women's Wisdom," untethered and flying free. A friend of mine pointed out that just as the hemorrhaging woman had been bleeding for twelve years, so have I been seeking God's inner healing for twelve years, ever since her story touched my life so deeply. Writing this book may be my way of touching Jesus' cloak!

Questions for Reflection:

> ➤ *God named himself to Moses at the burning bush, saying: "I am who I am." Who is God calling YOU to be in this season of your life?*

> ➤ *What might inner healing look like in your life?*

RAFT #4

Rafting Into The Future

Beloveds

*W*ith the intention of deepening my wellspring of wisdom, I am stepping into a new raft, as a participant in the Shalem Institute's "Spiritual Guidance Program," which will equip me to serve as a Spiritual Director for individuals who want companionship and guidance in listening to God's voice. Although Spiritual Direction is not widely practiced in the Presbyterian Church (USA), Shalem's ecumenical orientation welcomes spiritual leaders of all denominations to receive Spiritual Direction for themselves, so that they can more effectively offer direction to individuals, who have a desire to listen more deeply to God's voice within them.

One of my concerns for my denomination, as I have already expressed, is a lack of "pastoral care/spiritual direction" for ministers and leaders of congregations. If I can make myself available to ministers and leaders as a good listener, co-discerner of the Holy Spirit's wisdom, and spiritual companion and prayer partner, I would be grateful.

In addition, I feel called to empower women to listen to God's voice in their lives and to trust that wisdom, rather than relying on voices in the world around them, as they make critical, life-changing decisions for themselves and their families. My first Spiritual Director guided me in that way. I found that, despite all of my strong educational background, deep faith commitment, and confidence in my abilities, I tended to defer to others and to poll people whom I respected for advice, clarity and confirmation of what I already strongly felt God was leading me to do. Dr. Cindy Morgan, my Supervisor for the pilgrimage in Bangladesh, noticed my hesitation in trusting the Spirit's words within me.

While entering this new season of my life and ministry, the entire country and the world have been experiencing an extended "pause," because of the outbreak of Coronavirus, COVID 19, as a worldwide pandemic. It is the first time in my life that communities of faith have had to close their doors to regular worship services and gatherings of more than ten people. This government mandated shut-down, based on the recommendations of medical professionals around the world, is unprecedented and global. My prayers go out to all the families who have suffered loss at this time and to all medical professionals and other essential workers who put their lives at risk every day.

God's creation is groaning with sighs too deep for words. We have not taken proper care, nor exercised good stewardship of the planet: air, water, vegetation, animals and human life. Cosmic forces are slowing everyone down at the same time, bringing to our attention that all life is sacred and people of all cultures and faith traditions need one another. A sense of unity and kindness is being revealed, as people practice social distancing and work from home to protect the most vulnerable. No one knows how long this will last and what the long term impact will be on human lives, communities and nations. This is certainly a Class IV Rapids for the entire planet. As in all times of crisis, it is my prayer that this will be an opportunity for people to re-prioritize what is most important and to let go of what is not.

I am participating in an on-line book club, which is studying, *If Women Rose Rooted*, by Sharon Blackie, who delves deeply into the history of Celtic women, in what is now Ireland. She unearths a deep connection between women and the natural world. She calls them "the creators of life, the bearers of the cup of knowledge and wisdom, personifying the moral and spiritual authority of this fertile green and blue Earth."[41]

In the second chapter, she talks about "Wells and Waters." In ancient times the wells were guarded and tended by women. She highlights "the 'wellspring' of women's wisdom as a source of continual or abundant supply. Wells, along with certain rivers and lakes, have been recognized as sacred in nearly every culture on the planet and throughout every age."[42] Blackie talks about the fact that people and the land are intimately connected. "When we care for the land, it cares for us." [43] This is what maintains balance and health in the world.

Blackie goes on to say that "since the time of the industrial revolution and the rise of western civilization, humans have lost touch with the ancient wisdom."[44] The web of life and health has been broken. She attributes this to a devaluation of the feminine, who were the Voices of the Wells in Celtic history. She says, "we have lost the dark, dancing wisdom of women, their deep ways of knowing, their creative, life-giving fire."[45] Blackie urges women to be rooted, like trees, in the wellspring of God's abundance, which is deeply connected to the well-being of all creation. Her purpose for writing the book was to shift our conversations

---

[41] Sharon Blackie, *If Women Rose Rooted: The Journey to Authenticity and Belonging* (Sharon Blackie, copyrighted in September 2016), p. 5.

[42] Ibid., p. 23.

[43] Ibid., p. 30.

[44] Ibid., p. 34.

[45] Ibid.

away from a culture of blame towards a culture of healing, by utilizing the gifts of women and men in a healthy balance.

It was the women who stayed close to Jesus in his time of suffering, who arrived to anoint his body after his death, who were greeted by him outside the tomb. We must face the pain and the suffering of this world, not run from it. There are ways out of the wasteland, paths through the woods, which travel directly through the heart. Generations of women, grandmothers and mothers—many unnamed—raised both daughters and sons to be courageous, to make a difference, to lead people out of slavery into the promised land, to protect them from destruction, to experience healing, to transform the world by renewing creation, protecting the environment, practicing restraint and respecting all of God's children.

May our deepest desire be for God's Kingdom to come and God's will to be done on earth as it is in heaven. In God's peaceable kingdom, described by Isaiah,[46] the lions of the world will lie down with the lambs. In Eugene Peterson's Bible translation, *The Message*,[47] the last few verses of the passage say this: "Neither animal nor human will hurt or kill on my holy mountain. The whole earth will be brimming with knowing God-Alive, a living knowledge of God ocean-deep, ocean-wide." It is my desire to deepen my roots

---

[46] Isaiah 11:1-9.

[47] Eugene Peterson, *The Message*. (Colorado Springs, Colorado, NavPres, Tyndale House Publishers), 1993. It was Eugene Peterson's spiritual autobiography, *The Pastor: A Memoir*, (Colorado Springs, CO: Harper Collins Publishing), 2011, which inspired me to write my story about motherhood, mission and ministry.

in the wellspring of God's wisdom, and to do my small "piece" in restoring "peace" to God's creation.[48]

Questions for Reflection:

➢ *As the world pauses, what do you recognize as the most important priority in your life?*

➢ *How is God calling you to make a positive difference in your place in the world?*

---

[48] These words were inspired by Ally Markotich's art workshop, "Claiming our Piece… to Claim our Peace," offered to the leadership of Bethesda Presbyterian Church in August 2019.

ACKNOWLEDGEMENTS

First, I want to thank every person who has stayed on the raft with me through the rapids of my spiritual journey! I hope and pray that some of my questions connected with you, gave you food for thought, prayer, and also the assurance that you are not alone.

Second, I want to thank my angels of encouragement, who have believed in me as a writer and stood beside me in moments of fear and discouragement. I have learned that writing can be a lonely enterprise, and requires seclusion, concentration and focus, without a lot of direct feedback or affirmation along the way.

I thank my partner in life, David Hudson, for, as he would say, "I never put the 'kibosh' on anything you wanted to do or held you back from pursuing God's call in your life." And that is, oh, so true! I love you, honey, and thank you for allowing Sue to be Sue. That is easier said than done!

I thank my daughters for all I have learned from and with you during our years together. You are each gifted beyond measure, as different as night and day, and voices of wisdom in your own right. Rebekah, your technological expertise, entertainment coordination, great sense of humor, beautifully worded prayers, and deep empathy for all of us deserves applause. You are self-sacrificing and loving and once told me you are the "glue" that holds our family together. You have proven that many times. I am handing you a gold medal! As the first daughter, you do love being first!

Rachel, you have embodied some of my dreams, by pursuing cross-cultural immersion in Mexico, Chile, Argentina, Peru and Spain. I could not be more proud of your fluency in Spanish. It is music to my ears whenever I have the opportunity to hear you speak freely, translate conscientiously, and understand people in their own cultural context. Some of your closest friends, like you, have one foot in one culture and one foot in another. Your deep faith and commitment to God is a beautiful testimony to all who know you. God goes before you, as you seek to discern God's will for your future, one step at a time. Thank you for being a gifted translator, teacher, and a person who does not quit. You see things through to the end, even when they are difficult. I admire and love you so much.

Mary, my kindred spirit, who feels deeply, I am so proud of you for who you are and all you are doing to make the world a better place for everyone. Your time overseas in Pakistan, India, Rwanda, and France has only deepened your love and empathy for all people in the world. Your work with refugees and as a social worker goes above and beyond all expectations. Your family loves and admires your commitment to justice and change. You ARE the change people need to see in the world. Thank you for being Mary Elizabeth Hudson, your grandmother's namesake.

This book would not have been possible without the support of my long-time friend, Laura Gingerich. She took all of the pictures of the art work and the people represented in this book. Laura is known for "having an eye for beauty in the midst of chaos" from her work in Afghanistan, Lebanon, Haiti, Pakistan, West Bank and India. When Laura is not on assignment, she loves sharing her knowledge by leading photography workshops that inspire and motivate beginners to advanced level enthusiasts around the globe. Check out her website: www.lauragingerich.com.

Many family and friends have stuck by me through thick and thin. Thank you all for touching my life deeply and for having opened your hearts and homes to me: Robyn Decker, Laura Gingerich, Laura Murdock, Ally Markotich, Mary Gamble, Marilyn Wagner, Debbie and Marty Prince, Kathleen White, Adam Ruiz, Vivian and Bill Millar, Michelle Packard, Lisa Brisson, Drs. Cindy and Les Morgan, Shanti Devadas, and Rev. Nosheen Khan. In the hustle and bustle of your busy lives, you have been there for me. There are so many more people I could name from every chapter of my life. You know who you are: church members, professors, teachers, friends, counselors, fellow students, who are too many to name. Thank you for your on-going prayers, as well as your love and laughter all of these years. God's unconditional love for all of us is a wellspring that will never run dry! Virtual hugs to all!

I am finishing this book on April 12, 2020, the Easter Sunday when I had the privilege of sitting on our ocean-colored couches, between Rachel and David Hudson. I do not usually get to hold the pastor's hand while he is preaching, but today I did as we watched the pre-recorded worship service on television. This book is my offering of love to the One we both have sought to serve throughout our lives, to the One who holds the future of all creation, and to "the One who is a God of mercy."[49]

---

[49] The last phrase of Rev. David Hudson's Easter sermon, April 12, 2020.

ABOUT THE AUTHOR

Rev. Sue Hudson grew up in Pittsburgh, Pennsylvania. This is her story of how she has tried to walk with God throughout her life. Most of the details are included in the book itself. She graduated from Mt. Lebanon High School and attended Wake Forest University, where she majored in English with a secondary teaching certificate. Sue and her husband, David, have served as missionaries for the Presbyterian Church (USA) in South Korea, Pakistan and India. Sue is a Certified Christian Educator for the PCUSA and also an ordained minister of Word and Sacrament. She received her Doctor of Ministry at Louisville Presbyterian Theological Seminary and a Certificate in Spiritual Formation from Columbia Seminary in Decatur, Georgia. She and David have three beautiful and gifted daughters: Rebekah, Rachel and Mary. Sue is presently participating in the Shalem Institute's "Spiritual Guidance Program" and hopes to be a Spiritual Director in the next chapter of her unfolding faith journey.

CPSIA information can be obtained
at www.ICGtesting.com
Printed in the USA
LVHW071223050223
738641LV00004B/13